ocuments on the Nineteenth Century United Kingdom Constitution

DOCUMENTS ON THE NINETEENTH CENTURY UNITED KINGDOM CONSTITUTION

Edited by
Andrew Blick

Volume II
People, Parties, and Politicians

LONDON AND NEW YORK

First published 2024
by Routledge
4 Park Square, Milton Park, Abingdon, Oxon OX14 4RN

and by Routledge
605 Third Avenue, New York, NY 10158

Routledge is an imprint of the Taylor & Francis Group, an informa business

© 2024 selection and editorial matter, Andrew Blick; individual owners retain copyright in their own material.

The right of Andrew Blick to be identified as the author of the editorial material, and of the authors for their individual chapters, has been asserted in accordance with sections 77 and 78 of the Copyright, Designs and Patents Act 1988.

All rights reserved. No part of this book may be reprinted or reproduced or utilised in any form or by any electronic, mechanical, or other means, now known or hereafter invented, including photocopying and recording, or in any information storage or retrieval system, without permission in writing from the publishers.

Trademark notice: Product or corporate names may be trademarks or registered trademarks, and are used only for identification and explanation without intent to infringe.

British Library Cataloguing-in-Publication Data
A catalogue record for this book is available from the British Library

ISBN: 978-0-367-41759-8 (set)
ISBN: 978-0-367-41764-2 (Volume II) hbk
ISBN: 978-0-367-81614-8 (Volume II) ebk

DOI: 10.4324/9780367816148

Typeset in Times New Roman
by Apex CoVantage, LLC

CONTENTS

VOLUME II PEOPLE, PARTIES, AND POLITICIANS

Acknowledgments ix
General Introduction x
Introduction to Volume II: People, Parties, and Politicians xiv

PART 1
Perspectives 1

1 Extract from *A Vindication of the Rights of Woman* 3
  MARY WOLLSTONECRAFT

2 'Framework Bill' 5
  LORD BYRON

3 You Ask Me, Why, Tho' Ill at Ease 10
  ALFRED TENNYSON

4 *The British Constitution* 12
  KARL MARX

5 Speech at Crystal Palace 13
  BENJAMIN DISRAELI

6 'Concerning Government' 15
  WILLIAM MORRIS

7 Extract from *The Crisis of Liberalism: New Issues of Democracy* 19
  J. A. HOBSON

CONTENTS

PART 2
Campaigns and Groups   23

8 *Society for Constitutional Information*   25

9 *The London Corresponding Society's Regulations*   26

10 'Masque of Anarchy'   29
    PERCY BYSSHE SHELLEY

11 'The People's Charter – Petition'   44
    THOMAS DUNCOMBE

12 *Address of the Committee to the People of England*   51

13 Extract from *Secularism in Its Various Relations*   53
    CHARLES WATTS

14 *The Militant Methods of the NWSPU*   55
    CHRISTABEL PANKHURST

15 *The Struggle for Political Liberty*   60
    CHRYSTAL MACMILLAN

PART 3
Representation   63

16 'Admission of Baron de Rothschild'   65

17 'Indian Taxation'   71
    SIR MANCHERJEE BHOWNAGGREE

18 'Liquor Traffic (Restrictions)'   72
    VISCOUNTESS (NANCY) ASTOR

19 'Royal Parks and Pleasure Gardens'   76
    MARGARET WINTRINGHAM

20 'Debate on the Address'   77
    SHAPURJI SAKLATVALA

CONTENTS

21	'Debate on the Address' MARGARET BONDFIELD	82
22	'Housing (Revision of Contributions) Bill' ELEANOR RATHBONE	86
23	'Annual Holiday Bill' MARION PHILLIPS	90

PART 4
Rights and Freedoms   93

24	'Religious Liberty' CHARLES JAMES FOX	95
25	*A Habeas Corpus Suspension Act*, 1794	97
26	'The Case of Wolf Tone'	98
27	*Combination Act*, 1800	100
28	'Standing Order for the Exclusion of Strangers' RICHARD SHERIDAN	103
29	'Habeas Corpus Suspension Bill' SIR SAMUEL ROMILLY	108
30	*Repeal of the Test and Corporation Acts*, 1828	112
31	*Roman Catholic Emancipation Act*, 1829	115
32	'Newspaper Stamp Duties' EDWARD LYTTON BULWER	117
33	'Public Meetings in the Metropolis' CHARLES BRADLAUGH	123
34	(Industrial Action) Taff Vale Case, Decision of Mr. Justice Farewell	130

vii

CONTENTS

35 *Aliens Act*, 1905 — 134

36 'Trade Disputes Bill' — 137
   LORD LOREBURN

37 *Cinematograph Act*, 1909 — 143

38 *Official Secrets Act*, 1911 — 145

39 *Defence of the Realm Act*, 1914 — 148

40 *Emergency Powers Act*, 1920 — 149

41 *Report of the Broadcasting Committee*, 1925: Summary of Recommendations — 151

42 'Trade Disputes and Trade Unions Bill' — 153
   ELLEN WILKINSON

Index — 157

ACKNOWLEDGMENTS

I would like to thank Linda Colley for encouraging me to take on the task of editing these volumes; at Routledge, Rachel Douglas, Simon Alexander, and Sarahjayne Smith; and at Apex, Marie Roberts. The staff of the British Library were as helpful as ever. Robert Blackburn provided useful advice. As always, support came from my family members: Frederick, George, Nicola, Karen, Katharine and Robin Blick. I bear sole responsibility for the contents.

Andrew Blick
Acton, London
March 2023

GENERAL INTRODUCTION

This four-volume work seeks to present the reader with primary sources pertaining to the United Kingdom (UK) constitution during the period 1776–1928. This proposition raises a number of questions. First, what is a constitution? For the purposes of this work, I define it as the institutions of governance; the rules that apply to their operation; their interactions with each other; and their relationship with the public, collectively and individually. The bodies that come within this remit include the monarchy, the executive branch, Parliament, the courts, and local government. Famously, the UK has lacked what is known as a 'written' or 'codified' constitution (except perhaps in its pre-history in the era of Oliver Cromwell during the 1650s). Therefore there is no single, specific constitutional text which a work such as this can reproduce.

However, while there is no one document setting out the core features of the system, there is much relevant written material, for this period as for others. There are various Acts of Parliament, for instance, that provide a legal basis for aspects of the constitution (see e.g.: *An Act for the Union of Great Britain and Ireland*, 1800). Furthermore, the texts of various speeches and other documents seek to describe or establish principles or 'conventions': rules that, though 'softer' in nature than full legislation, can nonetheless have powerful political force and are crucial to the functioning of the system. Among them is the principle, emergent during the period under consideration, that a government should possess the 'confidence' of the House of Commons, the elected chamber of Parliament (see e.g.: 'Confidence in the Ministry', Sir Robert Peel, in the House of Commons, 27 May 1841).

Those purporting to describe those aspects of the constitution that were more political than legal in nature often did so through reference to precedent, seeking to ground themselves in the past. But the border of demarcation between the depiction of what *was* and what a given author thought *ought to be* could be blurred. In other instances, demands for change in the nature of the constitution were overt. They might involve calls for one ('Ought the Referendum to Be Introduced into England?', Albert Venn Dicey, *The Contemporary Review*, April 1890) or multiple (see e.g.: *Secularism in Its Various Relations*, Charles Watts, 1875) alterations. Demands for change could in turn be met by opposition (see e.g.: *Woman's Sphere*, Violet Markham, speech at Albert Hall, 28 February 1912).

GENERAL INTRODUCTION

In some instances, there have been challenges to the overall nature of the system and its authority rather than one aspect of it (see e.g.: *1916 Proclamation* [of the Provisional Government of the Irish Republic]), with – again – attempted refutations (see e.g.: *Village Politics*, Hannah More, 1792). Further projected constitutional projects have involved proposed constructions designed to add to more than supplant existing mechanisms (see e.g.: 'Report of the Special Committee of the League, Imperial Federation', *Journal of the Imperial Federation League*, 1 December 1892). Sources also offered general interpretations of the constitution and the way in which it functioned. They could be of more critical (see e.g.: *The British Constitution*, Karl Marx, 2 March 1855) or optimistic (see e.g.: 'You Ask Me Why, Tho' Ill at Ease', Alfred Tennyson, 1833) character.

What is the nature of the polity the constitution of which is under consideration? The UK consisted, since 1707 and up to 1801, of England – into which Wales was legally incorporated – and Scotland, making up the United Kingdom of Great Britain. The implementation in 1801 of legislation passed the previous year (*An Act for the Union of Great Britain and Ireland*, 1800) created the United Kingdom of Great Britain and Ireland. From the early 1920s change occurred again, with the departure of most of the island of Ireland to form what would eventually become the Republic of Ireland (see: *1921 Anglo Irish Treaty, Articles of Agreement*, as signed 6 December 1921). During this period, UK political institutions also asserted authority over territories dispersed across multiple continents. Issues involving the Empire and its governance could therefore engage the constitution of the UK and are given consideration in this work.

Why is the 1776–1928 time period used? Historians often take a flexible approach towards centuries. In this case, the nineteenth century takes a long form. The starting point is selected since it is the year of two important contributions to the cause of parliamentary and electoral reform ('Parliamentary Reform', John Wilkes, in the House of Commons, 21 March 1776; *Take Your Choice! Representation and Respect, Imposition and Contempt*, John Cartwright, 1776); and the revolt of the American colonies (*1776 American Declaration of Independence*). The choice of 1928 reflects that the year saw the passing of the fifth of the great reform acts of the period (*Representation of the People [Equal Franchise] Act*, 1928, Polling Districts and Places, 6 July 1928). This law marked the advent of a full adult franchise. The time span covered in these volumes, then, stretches from a point at which the idea of mass voting rights was coming onto the political agenda, to its wide realisation.

During this period various other features of the UK variant of democracy became established. They included the concept of a body of senior ministers, the Cabinet, drawn from Parliament, collectively and individually responsible for the conduct of government (see e.g.: 'Lord Ellenborough's Seat in the Cabinet', Lord Castlereagh, in the House of Commons, 3 March 1806). This committee, chaired by the holder of the increasingly recognised post of prime minister, became in practice the dominant body within the executive, with the monarch increasingly (though not wholly) becoming a figurehead more than a political leader (see e.g.:

The English Constitution, Walter Bagehot, 1867). The principle of Parliament being sovereign – that is, having supreme and unchecked legislative authority – though its roots long predated the nineteenth century, gained wide prominence, assisted in large part by the work of the jurist A. V. Dicey (*Introduction to the Study of the Law of the Constitution*, 1889 [Third Edition]). Within Parliament, the relationship between the House of Commons, the membership of which was determined by an expanding electorate, and the unelected House of Lords was increasingly a subject of scrutiny (see e.g.: 'Irish Church Bill', Lord Salisbury, in the House of Lords, 17 June 1869) and a source of dispute and instability (see e.g.: 'Education [England and Wales] Bill', Sir Henry Campbell-Bannerman, in the House of Lords, 20 December 1906). The primacy of the Commons over the Lords gained legislative expression in 1911 (*Parliament Act*, 1911). Developments, however, were not necessarily unilinear. For instance, there could be movement in the direction of individual freedom (see e.g.: *Roman Catholic Emancipation Act*, 1829) but also towards greater governmental interference (see e.g.: *Emergency Powers Act*, 1920). Furthermore, some paths were advocated – seriously considered even – but not taken at the time (see e.g.: *Machinery of Representation*, Thomas Hare, 1867).

What sources have been used? The work seeks a degree of diversity of various kinds. It draws upon parliamentary materials, legal proceedings, Acts of Parliament, public speeches, private correspondence, pamphlets, statements issued by organisations, treaties, official files, memoirs, and works of creative literature. There is a span of types of institutional author, from official bodies through to radical campaign organisations. For texts attributed to individuals, there has been an attempt to include those of varied profiles as far as possible given the constraints imposed by social realities of the time. A diversity of viewpoints – from the conservative, to the reformist, to the radical – is presented.

Finally, what specific subject areas have been chosen for each volume? Volume I: Reform focuses on rules pertaining to the composition of the House of Commons, campaigns to change them, and reforms that were introduced. It includes the matters of who could vote and the way in which they did so, how votes should be counted, the territorial distribution of representatives, who could sit in the House of Commons, the resources available to them, and when elections should take place, as well as more radical proposals for mass involvement in specific decisions. Volume II: People, Parties, and Politicians engages with the politics of the constitution, how individuals were able to operate individually and collectively within the system, and the way in which they were represented. It provides a range of perspectives and analyses significant to the constitution and contains sources relevant to the operation of various groups and campaigns of constitutional significance. The volume presents material relevant to the inclusion of previously excluded groups within Parliament and to the attainment and restriction of rights and freedoms.

Volume III: Institutions deals with various official bodies relevant to the operation of the constitution: the monarchy, the prime minister, the Cabinet, administrations as a whole and their mandates, the Civil Service and the machinery of government, Parliament and within that the relationship between the House of Commons and the House of Lords, local government, and the courts and legal system. Volume IV: Nations and Empire deals with the constitutional aspects of the UK as a state in its internal configuration and external interactions. It covers the significance of American independence and the impact of the French revolution. The volume presents sources pertaining to constitutional aspects of the external role of the UK as a major imperial power. It then includes material relevant to the multi-national makeup of the state and various approaches proposed and followed in managing this status.

The volumes do not purport to offer comprehensive accounts of their subject matter, nor realistically could they do so. Not every source which presents a given argument is necessarily representative of the balance of opinion on a given subject, or even of the particular cause with which it might be associated. Some of the opinions and values presented will be found objectionable by the reader: such content is included because it was being promulgated at the time. Entries are chosen because they provide insight into the nature and operation of the constitution and because they convey information or perspectives effectively and (at least relatively) succinctly.

INTRODUCTION TO VOLUME II
People, Parties, and Politicians

This volume engages with the politics of the constitution, how individuals were able to operate individually and collectively within the system, and the way in which they were represented. It provides a range of perspectives and analyses significant to the constitution and contains sources relevant to the operation of various groups and campaigns of constitutional significance. It presents material relevant to the inclusion of previously excluded groups within Parliament and to the attainment and restriction of rights and freedoms. Part 1 pertains to attempts by observers and activists to characterise the system and the way in which it changes, from a variety of different standpoints. They include the demand for women to be included within the political community (*A Vindication of the Rights of Woman*, Mary Wollstonecraft, 1792) and differing perspectives provided by two of the most esteemed poets of their day ('Framework Bill', Lord Byron, in the House of Lords, 27 February 1812; 'You Ask Me Why, Tho' Ill at Ease', Alfred Tennyson, 1833). There is a revolutionary, communist perspective (*The British Constitution*, Karl Marx, 2 March 1855) and a Conservative outlook (Speech at Crystal Palace, Benjamin Disraeli, 24 June 1872). Another creative artist, in depicting an idealised society of the future, provides a critique of then-present arrangements ('Concerning Government', William Morris, *News from Nowhere*, 1890). A radical Liberal view follows (*The Crisis of Liberalism: New Issues of Democracy*, J. A. Hobson, 1909).

Part 2 contains material generated by various organisations and movements. It includes texts produced by some of the earliest groups that prefigured later drives for franchise expansion (*Society for Constitutional Information*, 1783; *The London Corresponding Society's Regulations*, London, 24 May 1792). The 1819 'Peterloo massacre' of participants in a rally for parliamentary reform in Manchester inspired a work of poetry, which the authorities attempted to supress for some time, by an author who came to be widely read among reform campaigners ('Masque of Anarchy', Percy Bysshe Shelley, 1819). A group formed in response to perceived administrative inefficiency developed a programme more expansive and radical than this trigger might suggest it would be (*Address of the Committee to the People of England*, Administrative Reform Association, 19 May 1855). Similarly, support for secularism – that is, the separation of the public and religious spheres – could connect to an extensive set of objectives (*Secularism in its Various Relations*, Charles Watts, 1875). There is evidence of various campaigns at work in seeking to pressure lawmakers to expand the right to vote (see e.g.: *The Militant Methods of the NWSPU*, Christabel Pankhurst, speech at St. James's Hall, 15 October 1908).

Part 3 provides sources reflecting the impact made by greater diversity of membership in the House of Commons. The examples are selective rather than complete, chosen because they convey particular points precisely. They illustrate the immediate challenge to established arrangements posed by the introduction of a Jewish MP ('Admission of Baron de Rothschild', in the House of Commons of Commons, 26 July 1858) and the distinctive contribution that came from two MPs of Indian heritage ('Indian Taxation', Sir Mancherjee Bhownaggree, in the House of Commons, 3 September 1895; 'Debate on the Address', Shapurji Saklatvala, in the House of Commons, 23 November 1922). Extended coverage is given to women – who were formally barred from entry to Parliament before 1918 – and their particular input into Commons proceedings (see e.g.: 'Annual Holiday Bill', Marion Phillips, in the House of Commons, 15 November 1929).

Part 4 deals with controversies pertaining to a range of rights, including of assembly ('Public Meetings in the Metropolis', Charles Bradlaugh, in the House of Commons, 1 March 1888) and association ('Trade Disputes and Trade Unions Bill', Ellen Wilkinson, in the House of Commons, 5 May 1927). Among the measures and decisions documented, some were supportive of freedoms, such as that of religious belief (see e.g.: *Repeal of the Test and Corporation Acts*, 1828), while others were of restrictive nature over matters including security of the person (see e.g.: *A Habeas Corpus Suspension Act*, 1794). Freedom of the press, including the ability to report parliamentary proceedings, was a prominent subject of contention (see e.g.: 'Standing Order for the Exclusion of Strangers', Richard Sheridan, in the House of Commons, 6 February 1810). Towards the end of the period, new media – cinema and broadcasting – had appeared, which prompted further regulation and policy (*Cinematograph Act*, 1909; *Report of the Broadcasting Committee*, 1925, Summary of Recommendations).

Part 1

PERSPECTIVES

1

EXTRACT FROM *A VINDICATION OF THE RIGHTS OF WOMAN*

Mary Wollstonecraft

Source: *A Vindication of the Rights of Woman*, 1792, pp. 66–67

Contending for the rights of woman, my main argument is built on this simple principle, that if she be not prepared by education to become the companion of man, she will stop the progress of knowledge and virtue; for truth must be common to all, or it will be inefficacious with respect to its influence on general practice. And how can woman be expected to co-operate unless she know why she ought to be virtuous? unless freedom strengthen her reason till she comprehend her duty, and see in what manner it is connected with her real good? If children are to be educated to understand the true principle of patriotism, their mother must be a patriot; and the love of mankind, from which an orderly train of virtues spring, can only be produced by considering the moral and civil interest of mankind; but the education and situation of woman, at present, shuts her out from such investigations.

In this work I have produced many arguments, which to me were conclusive, to prove that the prevailing notion respecting a sexual character was subversive of morality, and I have contended, that to render the human body and mind more perfect, chastity must more universally prevail, and that chastity will never be respected in the male world till the person of a woman is not, as it were, idolized, when little virtue or sense embellish it with the grand traces of mental beauty, or the interesting simplicity of affection.

Consider, Sir, dispassionately, these observations – for a glimpse of this truth seemed to open before you when you observed, 'that to see one half of the human race excluded by the other from all participation of government, was a political phaenomenon that, according to abstract principles, it was impossible to explain.' If so, on what does your constitution rest? If the abstract rights of man will bear discussion and explanation, those of woman, by a parity of reasoning, will not shrink from the same test: though a different opinion prevails in this country, built on the very arguments which you use to justify the oppression of woman – prescription.

Consider, I address you as a legislator, whether, when men contend for their freedom, and to be allowed to judge for themselves respecting their own happiness, it be not inconsistent and unjust to subjugate women, even though you firmly believe that you are acting in the manner best calculated to promote their happiness? Who made man the exclusive judge, if woman partake with him the gift of reason?

In this style, argue tyrants of every denomination, from the weak king to the weak father of a family; they are all eager to crush reason; yet always assert that they usurp its throne only to be useful. Do you not act a similar part, when you *force* all women, by denying them civil and political rights, to remain immured in their families groping in the dark? for surely, Sir, you will not assert, that a duty can be binding which is not founded on reason? If indeed this be their destination, arguments may be drawn from reason: and thus augustly supported, the more understanding women acquire, the more they will be attached to their duty – comprehending it – for unless they comprehend it, unless their morals be fixed on the same immutable principle as those of man, no authority can make them discharge it in a virtuous manner. They may be convenient slaves, but slavery will have its constant effect, degrading the master and the abject dependent.

But, if women are to be excluded, without having a voice, from a participation of the natural rights of mankind, prove first, to ward off the charge of injustice and inconsistency, that they want reason – else this flaw in your NEW CONSTITUTION will ever shew that man must, in some shape, act like a tyrant, and tyranny, in whatever part of society it rears its brazen front, will ever undermine morality.

2

'FRAMEWORK BILL'

Lord Byron

Source: House of Lords, 27 February 1812

My Lords; the subject now submitted to your lordships for the first time, though new to the House, is by no means new to the country. I believe it had occupied the serious thoughts of all descriptions of persons, long before its introduction to the notice of that legislature, whose interference alone could be of real service. As a person in some degree connected with the suffering county, though a stranger not only to this House in general, but to almost every individual whose attention I presume to solicit, I must claim some portion of your lordships' indulgence, whilst I offer a few observations on a question in which I confess myself deeply interested.

To enter into any detail of the Riots would be superfluous: the House is already aware that every outrage short of actual bloodshed has been perpetrated, and that the proprietors of the Frames obnoxious to the rioters, and all persons supposed to be connected with them, have been liable to insult and violence. During the short time I recently passed in Nottinghamshire, not twelve hours elapsed without some fresh act of violence; and on the day I left the county I was informed that forty frames had been broken the preceding evening, as usual, without resistance and without detection.

Such was then the state of that county, and such I have reason to believe it to be at this moment. But whilst these outrages must be admitted to exist to an alarming extent, it cannot be denied that they have arisen from circumstances of the most unparalleled distress: The perseverance of these miserable men in their proceedings, tends to prove that nothing but absolute want could have driven a large, and once honest and industrious, body of the people, into the commission of excesses so hazardous to themselves, their families and the community. At the time, to which I allude, the town and county were burthened with large detachments of the military; the police was in motion, the magistrates assembled, yet all the movements civil and military had led to – nothing. Not a single instance had occurred of the apprehension of any real delinquent actually taken in the fact, against whom there existed legal evidence sufficient for conviction. But the police, however useless, were by no means idle: several notorious delinquents had been detected; men, liable to conviction, on the clearest evidence, of the capital crime of Poverty; men, who had been nefariously guilty of lawfully begetting several children, whom, thanks to the times they were unable to maintain. Considerable injury has been done to the proprietors of the improved Frames. These machines were to them an advantage, inasmuch as they superseded the necessity of employing a number of workmen, who were left in consequence to starve. By the adoption of one species of Frame in particular, one man performed the work of many, and the superfluous labourers were thrown out of employment. Yet it is to be observed, that the work thus executed was inferior in quality; not marketable at home, and merely hurried over with a view to exportation. It was called in the cant of the trade, by the name of 'Spider work.' The rejected workmen in the blindness of their ignorance, instead of rejoicing at these improvements in arts so beneficial to mankind, conceived themselves to be sacrificed to improvements in mechanism. In the foolishness of their hearts they imagined, that the maintenance and well doing of the industrious poor, were objects of greater consequence than the enrichment of a few individuals by any improvement, in the implements of trade, which threw the workmen out of employment, and rendered the labourer unworthy of his hire. And it must be confessed that although the adoption of the enlarged machinery in that state of our commerce which the country once boasted, might have been beneficial to the master without being detrimental to the servant; yet, in the present situation of our manufactures, rotting in warehouses, without a prospect of exportation, with the demand for work and workmen equally diminished; Frames of this description, tend materially to aggravate the distress and discontent of the disappointed sufferers. But the real cause of these distresses and consequent disturbances lies deeper. When we are told that these men are leagued together not only for the destruction of their own comfort, but of their very means of subsistence, can we forget that it is the bitter policy, the destructive warfare of the last 18 years, which has destroyed their comfort, your comfort, all mens' comfort? That policy, which, originating with "great statesmen now no more," has survived the dead to become a curse on the living, unto the third and fourth generation! These men never destroyed their looms till they were become useless, worse than useless; till they were become actual impediments to their exertions in obtaining their daily bread. Can you, then, wonder that in times like these, when bankruptcy, convicted fraud, and imputed felony are found in a station not far beneath that of your lordships, the lowest, though once most useful portion of the people should forget their duty in their distresses, and become only less guilty than one of their representatives? But while the exalted offender can find means to baffle the law, new capital punishments must be devised, new snares of death must be spread for the wretched mechanic who is famished into guilt. These men were willing to dig, but the spade was in other hands: they were not ashamed to beg, but there was none to relieve them: their own means of subsistence were cut off, all other employments pre-occupied, and their excesses, however to be deplored and condemned, can hardly be subject of surprize.

It has been stated that the persons in the temporary possession of Frames connive at their destruction; if this be proved upon enquiry, it were necessary that such material accessories to the crime, should be principals in the punishment. But I did hope, that any measure proposed by his Majesty's government, for your lordships' decision, would have had conciliation for its basis; or, if that were hopeless, that some previous enquiry, some deliberation would have been deemed requisite; not that we should have been called at once without examination, and without cause, to pass sentences by wholesale, and sign death-warrants blindfold. But, admitting that these men had no cause of complaint; that the grievances of them and their employers were alike groundless; that they deserved the worst; what inefficiency, what imbecility has been evinced in the method chosen to reduce them! Why were the military called out to be made a mockery of, if they were to be called out at all? As far as the difference of seasons would permit, they have merely parodied the summer campaign of major Sturgeon; and, indeed, the whole proceedings, civil and military, seemed on the model of those of the Mayor and Corporation of Garratt. – Such marchings and counter marchings! from Nottingham to Bullwell, from Bullwell to Banford, from Banford to Mansfield! and when at length the detachments arrived at their destination, in all "the pride, pomp, and circumstance of glorious war," they came just in time to witness the mischief which had been done, and ascertain the escape of the perpetrators, to collect the "spolia opima" in the fragments of broken frames, and return to their quarters amidst the derision of old women, and the hootings of children. Now, though in a free country, it were to be wished, that our military should never be too formidable, at least to ourselves, I cannot see the policy of placing them in situations where they can only be made ridiculous. As the sword is the worst argument that can be used, so should it be the last. In this instance it has been the first; but providentially as yet only in the scabbard. The present measure will, indeed, pluck it from the sheath; yet had proper meetings been held in the earlier stages of these riots, had the grievances of these men and their masters (for they also had their grievances) been fairly weighed and justly examined, I do think that means might have been devised to restore these workmen to their avocations, and tranquillity to the county. At present the county suffers from the double infliction of an idle military and a starving population. In what state of apathy have we been plunged so long, that now for the first time the House has been officially apprized of these disturbances? All this has been transacting within 130 miles of London, and yet we, "good easy men, have deemed full sure our greatness was a ripening," and have sat down to enjoy our foreign triumphs in the midst of domestic calamity. But all the cities you have taken, all the armies which have retreated before your leaders are but paltry subjects of self congratulation, if your land divides against itself, and your dragoons and your executioners must be let loose against your fellow citizens. – You call these men a mob, desperate, dangerous, and ignorant; and seem to think that the only way to quiet the "Bellua multorum capitum" is to lop off a few of its superfluous heads, – But even a mob may be better reduced to reason by a mixture of conciliation and firmness, than by additional irritation and redoubled penalties. Are we aware of our obligations to a mob? It is the mob that labour in your fields and serve in your houses, that man your navy, and recruit your army, that have enabled you to defy all the world, and can also defy you when neglect and calamity have driven them to despair. You may call the people a mob, but do not forget, that a mob too often speaks the sentiments of the people. And here I must remark with what alacrity you are accustomed to fly to the succour of your distrest allies, leaving the distressed of your own country to the care of Providence or – the Parish. When the Portuguese suffered under the retreat of the French every arm was stretched out, every band was opened, from the rich man's largess, to the widow's mite, all was bestowed to enable them to rebuild their villages and replenish their granaries. And at this moment, when thousands of misguided but most unfortunate fellow-countrymen are struggling with the extremes of hardships and hunger, as your charity began abroad it should end at home. A much less sum, a tithe of the bounty bestowed on Portugal, even if those men (which I cannot admit without enquiry) could not have been restored to their employments, would have rendered unnecessary the tender mercies of the bayonet and the gibbet. But doubtless our friends have too many foreign claims to admit a prospect of domestic relief; though never did such objects demand it. I have traversed the seat of war in the peninsula, I have been in some of the most oppressed provinces of Turkey, but never under the most despotic of infidel governments did I behold such squalid wretchedness as I have seen since my return in the very heart of a Christian country. And what are your remedies? After months of inaction, and months of action worse than inactivity, at length comes forth the grand specific, the never failing nostrum of all state physicians, from the days of Draco to the present time. After feeling the pulse and shaking the head over the patient, prescribing the usual course of warm water and bleeding, the warm water of your maukish police, and the lancets of your military, these convulsions must terminate in death, the sure consummation of the prescriptions of all political Sangrados. Setting aside the palpable injustice and the certain inefficiency of the Bill, are there not capital punishments sufficient in your statutes? Is there not blood enough upon your penal code that more must be poured forth to ascend to Heaven and testify against you? How will you carry the Bill into effect? Can you commit a whole county to their own prisons? Will you erect a gibbet in every field and hang up men like scarecrows? or will you proceed (as you must to bring this measure into effect) by decimation? place the county under martial law? depopulate and lay waste all around you? and restore Sherwood forest as an acceptable gift to the crown, in its former condition of a royal chase and an asylum for outlaws? Are these the remedies for a starving and desperate populace? Will the famished wretch who has braved your bayonets, be appalled by your gibbets? When death is a relief, and the only relief it appears that you will afford him; will he be dragooned into tranquillity? Will that which could not be effected by your grenadiers, be accomplished by your executioners? If you proceed by the forms of law where is your evidence? Those who have refused to impeach their accomplices, when transportation only was the punishment, will hardly be tempted to witness against them when death is the penalty. With all due deference to the noble lords opposite, I think a little investigation, some previous enquiry would induce even them to change their purpose. That most favourite state measure, so marvellously efficacious in many and recent instances, temporizing, would not be without its advantages in this. When a proposal is made to emancipate or relieve, you hesitate, you deliberate for years, you temporise and tamper with the minds of men; but a death-bill must be passed offhand, without a thought of the consequences. Sure I am from what I have heard, and from what I have seen, that to pass the Bill under all the existing circumstances, without enquiry, without deliberation, would only be to add injustice to irritation, and barbarity to neglect. The framers of such a Bill must be content to inherit the honours of that Athenian lawgiver whose edicts were said to be written not in ink but in blood. But suppose it past; suppose one of these men, as I have seen them, – meagre with famine, sullen with despair, careless of a life which your lordships are perhaps about to value at something less than the price of a stocking-frame – suppose this man surrounded by the children for whom he is unable to procure bread at the hazard of his existence, about to be torn for ever from a family which he lately supported in peaceful industry, and which it is not his fault that he can no longer so support, suppose this man, and there are ten thousand such from whom you may select your Victims, dragged into court, to be tried for this new offence, by this new law; still, there are two things wanting to convict and condemn him; and these are, in my opinion, – Twelve Butchers for a Jury, and a Jefferies for a Judged!

3

YOU ASK ME, WHY, THO' ILL AT EASE

Alfred Tennyson

Source: You Ask Me, Why, Tho' Ill at Ease, 1833

You ask me, why, tho' ill at ease,
Within this region I subsist,
Whose spirits falter in the mist,
And languish for the purple seas?

It is the land that freemen till,
That sober-suited Freedom chose,
The land, where girt with friends or foes
A man may speak the thing he will;

A land of settled government,
A land of just and old renown,
Where Freedom slowly broadens down
From precedent to precedent:

Where faction seldom gathers head,
But by degrees to fullness wrought,
The strength of some diffusive thought
Hath time and space to work and spread.

Should banded unions persecute
Opinion, and induce a time
When single thought is civil crime,
And individual freedom mute;

Tho' Power should make from land to land
The name of Britain trebly great –
Tho' every channel of the State
Should almost choke with golden sand –

Yet waft me from the harbour-mouth,
Wild wind! I seek a warmer sky,
And I will see before I die
The palms and temples of the South.

4

THE BRITISH CONSTITUTION

Karl Marx

Source: *The British Constitution*, 2 March 1855, in Karl Marx and Frederick Engels, *Articles on Britain*, 1975

But what is the British Constitution? Does its essence lie in a representative system and a limitation of the power of the executive? These features distinguish it neither from the Constitution of the United States of North America nor from the constitutions of the numerous British joint-stock companies which know "their business". The British Constitution is, in fact, merely an out-of-date, superannuated, obsolete compromise between the bourgeoisie, who are *not officially* but actually *ruling* in all decisive spheres of bourgeois society, and the landed aristocracy, who are *governing officially*. Originally, after the "glorious" revolution of 1688, only a section of the bourgeoisie, the *financial aristocracy*, was included in the compromise. The Reform Bill of 1831 admitted another section, the *millocracy*, as the English call them, that is, the high dignitaries of the *industrial* bourgeoisie. The history of legislation since 1831 is the history of concessions made to the industrial bourgeoisie, ranging from the Poor Law to the repeal of the Corn Laws, and from the repeal of the Corn Laws to the death-duties on real estate.

If the bourgeoisie – even only the top layer of the middle classes – has been generally recognised as the *ruling class* in *political respects*, this has been done only on the condition that the entire administration in all details, even the executive functions of legislative power, that is, the actual legislation in both Houses of Parliament, should remain in the hands of the landed aristocracy. In the 1830s the bourgeoisie preferred the renewal of the compromise with the landed aristocracy to a compromise with the mass of the English people. The aristocracy, subjected to certain principles laid down by the bourgeoisie, now ruled exclusively in the Cabinet, in Parliament, in the Administration, in the Army and the Navy; this one half, and relatively the most important half, of the British nation is now compelled to sign its own death sentence, and to admit in the eyes of the whole world that it no longer has the ability to rule England. We only need to consider the attempts to galvanise its corpse. Cabinet upon cabinet is being formed only to dissolve itself after a few weeks in office. The crisis is permanent, the government only provisional. All political activity is suspended, and everyone admits that he is only thinking of how to lubricate the political machine sufficiently to prevent it from coming to a complete halt. The House of Commons no longer recognises itself in the cabinets created in its own image.

5

SPEECH AT CRYSTAL PALACE

Benjamin Disraeli

Source: Speech at Crystal Palace, 24 June 1872

Gentlemen, the Tory party, unless it is a national party, is nothing. It is not a confederacy of nobles, it is not a democratic multitude; it is a party formed from all the numerous classes in the realm – classes alike and equal before the law, but whose different conditions and different aims give vigour and variety to our national life.

Gentlemen, a body of public men distinguished by their capacity took advantage of these circumstances. They seized the helm of affairs in a manner the honour of which I do not for a moment question, but they introduced a new system into our political life. Influenced in a great degree by the philosophy and the politics of the Continent, they endeavoured to substitute cosmopolitan for national principles; and they baptized the new scheme of politics with the plausible name of 'Liberalism'. Far be it from me for a moment to intimate that a country like England should not profit by the political experience of Continental nations of not inferior civilization; far be it from me for a moment to maintain that the party which then obtained power and which has since generally possessed it did not make many suggestions for our public life that were of great value, and bring forward many measures which, though changes, were nevertheless improvements. But the tone and tendency of Liberalism cannot be long concealed. It is to attack the institutions of the country under the name of Reform, and to make war on the manners and customs of the people of this country under the pretext of Progress. During the forty years that have elapsed since the commencement of this new system – although the superficial have seen upon its surface only the contentions of political parties – the real state of affairs has been this: the attempt of one party to establish in this country cosmopolitan ideas, and the efforts of another – unconscious efforts, sometimes, but always continued – to recur to and resume those national principles to which they attribute the greatness and glory of the country.

The Liberal party cannot complain that they have not had fair play. Never had a political party such advantages, never such opportunities. They are still in power; they have been for a long period in power. And yet what is the result? I speak not I am sure the language of exaggeration when I say that they are viewed by the community with distrust and, I might even say, with repugnance. And, now, what is the

DOI: 10.4324/9780367816148-6

present prospect of the national party? I have ventured to say that in my opinion Liberalism, from its essential elements, notwithstanding all the energy and ability with which its tenets have been advocated by its friends – notwithstanding the advantage which has accrued to them, as I will confess, from all the mistakes of their opponents, is viewed by the country with distrust. Now in what light is the party of which we are members viewed by the country, and what relation does public opinion bear to our opinions and our policy? . . .

Now, I have always been of opinion that the Tory party has three great objects. The first is to maintain the institutions of the country – not from any sentiment of political superstition, but because we believe that they embody the principles upon which a community like England can alone safely rest. The principles of liberty, of order, of law, and of religion ought not to be entrusted to individual opinion or to the caprice and passion of multitudes, but should be embodied in a form of permanence and power. We associate with the monarchy the ideas which it represents – the majesty of law, the administration of justice, the fountain of mercy and of honour. We know that in the estates of the realm and the privileges they enjoy, is the best security for public liberty and good government. We believe that a national profession of faith can only be maintained by an established Church, and that no society is safe unless there is a public recognition of the providential government of the world, and of the future responsibility of man. Well, it is a curious circumstance that during all these same forty years of triumphant Liberalism, every one of these institutions has been attacked and assailed – I say, continuously attacked and assailed. And what, gentlemen, has been the result? For the last forty years the most depreciating comparisons have been instituted between the sovereignty of England and the sovereignty of a great republic. We have been called upon in every way, in Parliament, in the press, by articles in newspapers, by pamphlets, by every means which can influence opinion, to contrast the simplicity and economy of the sovereignty of the United States with the cumbrous cost of the sovereignty of England . . .

Now, if you consider the state of public opinion with regard to those estates of the realm, what do you find? Take the case of the House of Lords. The House of Lords has been assailed during this reign of Liberalism in every manner and unceasingly. Its constitution has been denounced as anomalous, its influence declared pernicious; but what has been the result of this assault and criticism of forty years? Why, the people of England, in my opinion, have discovered that the existence of a second chamber is necessary to constitutional government; and, while necessary to constitutional government, is, at the same time, of all political inventions the most difficult. Therefore, the people of this country have congratulated themselves that, by the aid of an ancient and famous history, there has been developed in this country an assembly which possesses all the virtues which a senate should possess – independence, great local influence, eloquence, all the accomplishments of political life, and a public training which no theory could supply.

6

'CONCERNING GOVERNMENT'

William Morris

Source: *News From Nowhere*, 1890

CHAPTER XI: CONCERNING GOVERNMENT

"Now," said I, "I have come to the point of asking questions which I suppose will be dry for you to answer and difficult for you to explain; but I have foreseen for some time past that I must ask them, will I 'nill I. What kind of a government have you? Has republicanism finally triumphed? or have you come to a mere dictatorship, which some persons in the nineteenth century used to prophesy as the ultimate outcome of democracy? Indeed, this last question does not seem so very unreasonable, since you have turned your Parliament House into a dung-market. Or where do you house your present Parliament?"

The old man answered my smile with a hearty laugh, and said: "Well, well, dung is not the worst kind of corruption; fertility may come of that, whereas mere dearth came from the other kind, of which those walls once held the great supporters. Now, dear guest, let me tell you that our present parliament would be hard to house in one place, because the whole people is our parliament."

"I don't understand," said I.

"No, I suppose not," said he. "I must now shock you by telling you that we have no longer anything which you, a native of another planet, would call a government."

"I am not so much shocked as you might think," said I, "as I know something about governments. But tell me, how do you manage, and how have you come to this state of things?"

Said he: "It is true that we have to make some arrangements about our affairs, concerning which you can ask presently; and it is also true that everybody does not always agree with the details of these arrangements; but, further, it is true that a man no more needs an elaborate system of government, with its army, navy, and police, to force him to give way to the will of the majority of his *equals*, than he wants a similar machinery to make him understand that his head and a stone wall cannot occupy the same space at the same moment. Do you want further explanation?"

"Well, yes, I do," quoth I.

Old Hammond settled himself in his chair with a look of enjoyment which rather alarmed me, and made me dread a scientific disquisition: so I sighed and abided. He said: "I suppose you know pretty well what the process of government was in the bad old times?"

"I am supposed to know," said I.

(Hammond) What was the government of those days? Was it really the Parliament or any part of it?

(I) No.

(H.) Was not the Parliament on the one side a kind of watch-committee sitting to see that the interests of the Upper Classes took no hurt; and on the other side a sort of blind to delude the people into supposing that they had some share in the management of their own affairs?

(I) History seems to show us this.

(H.) To what extent did the people manage their own affairs?

(I) I judge from what I have heard that sometimes they forced the Parliament to make a law to legalise some alteration which had already taken place.

(H.) Anything else?

(I) I think not. As I am informed, if the people made any attempt to deal with the *cause* of their grievances, the law stepped in and said, this is sedition, revolt, or what not, and slew or tortured the ringleaders of such attempts.

(H.) If Parliament was not the government then, nor the people either, what was the government?

(I) Can you tell me?

(H.) I think we shall not be far wrong if we say that government was the Law-Courts, backed up by the executive, which handled the brute force that the deluded people allowed them to use for their own purposes; I mean the army, navy, and police.

(I) Reasonable men must needs think you are right.

(H.) Now as to those Law-Courts. Were they places of fair dealing according to the ideas of the day? Had a poor man a good chance of defending his property and person in them?

(I) It is a commonplace that even rich men looked upon a law-suit as a dire misfortune, even if they gained the case; and as for a poor one – why, it was considered a miracle of justice and beneficence if a poor man who had once got into the clutches of the law escaped prison or utter ruin.

(H.) It seems, then, my son, that the government by law-courts and police, which was the real government of the nineteenth century, was not a great success even to the people of that day, living under a class system which proclaimed inequality and poverty as the law of God and the bond which held the world together.

(I) So it seems, indeed.

(H.) And now that all this is changed, and the "rights of property," which mean the clenching the fist on a piece of goods and crying out to the neighbours, You shan't have this! – now that all this has disappeared so utterly that it is no longer possible even to jest upon its absurdity, is such a Government possible?

(I) It is impossible.

(H.) Yes, happily. But for what other purpose than the protection of the rich from the poor, the strong from the weak, did this Government exist?

(I.) I have heard that it was said that their office was to defend their own citizens against attack from other countries.

(H.) It was said; but was anyone expected to believe this? For instance, did the English Government defend the English citizen against the French?

(I) So it was said.

(H.) Then if the French had invaded England and conquered it, they would not have allowed the English workmen to live well?

(I, laughing) As far as I can make out, the English masters of the English workmen saw to that: they took from their workmen as much of their livelihood as they dared, because they wanted it for themselves.

(H.) But if the French had conquered, would they not have taken more still from the English workmen?

(I) I do not think so; for in that case the English workmen would have died of starvation; and then the French conquest would have ruined the French, just as if the English horses and cattle had died of under-feeding. So that after all, the English *workmen* would have been no worse off for the conquest: their French Masters could have got no more from them than their English masters did.

(H.) This is true; and we may admit that the pretensions of the government to defend the poor (*i.e.*, the useful) people against other countries come to nothing. But that is but natural; for we have seen already that it was the function of government to protect the rich against the poor. But did not the government defend its rich men against other nations?

(I) I do not remember to have heard that the rich needed defence; because it is said that even when two nations were at war, the rich men of each nation gambled with each other pretty much as usual, and even sold each other weapons wherewith to kill their own countrymen.

(H.) In short, it comes to this, that whereas the so-called government of protection of property by means of the law-courts meant destruction of wealth, this defence of the citizens of one country against those of another country by means of war or the threat of war meant pretty much the same thing.

(I) I cannot deny it.

(H.) Therefore the government really existed for the destruction of wealth?

(I) So it seems. And yet –

(H.) Yet what?

(I) There were many rich people in those times.

(H.) You see the consequences of that fact?

(I) I think I do. But tell me out what they were.

(H.) If the government habitually destroyed wealth, the country must have been poor?

(I) Yes, certainly.

(H.) Yet amidst this poverty the persons for the sake of whom the government existed insisted on being rich whatever might happen?

(I.) So it was.

(H.) What must happen if in a poor country some people insist on being rich at the expense of the others?

(I.) Unutterable poverty for the others. All this misery, then, was caused by the destructive government of which we have been speaking?

(H.) Nay, it would be incorrect to say so. The government itself was but the necessary result of the careless, aimless tyranny of the times; it was but the machinery of tyranny. Now tyranny has come to an end, and we no longer need such machinery; we could not possibly use it since we are free. Therefore in your sense of the word we have no government. Do you understand this now?

7

EXTRACT FROM *THE CRISIS OF LIBERALISM: NEW ISSUES OF DEMOCRACY*

J. A. Hobson

Source: *The Crisis of Liberalism: New Issues of Democracy*, 1909, pp. 11–15

Were the proposed destruction of the Lords' veto to leave the House of Commons vested with supreme authority of government, a large stride towards effective democracy might seem to have been taken. By securing an extended franchise, shorter parliaments and adequate reforms of electoral machinery, the representative assembly might at least become a genuine expression of the popular will. There would no doubt be many even among Liberals, distrustful of uni-cameral government, where the absence of a written constitution would confer upon a single chamber, possibly elected on some heated party issue, an unlimited power to change the very foundations and fabric of government. But this danger is under the present system greatly enhanced by the fact that the mere abolition of the veto would establish not the supremacy of the House of Commons, but a Cabinet autocracy qualified in certain electoral conditions by the power of some enclave or "cave" in a party. There are circumstances under which this state of affairs might easily lead to Cæsarism, where a magnetic party leader either succeeded in capturing the imagination of the populace or in engineering a supremacy among competing politicians.

The consideration of the wider issues of democracy cannot be postponed. Though in pursuance of our customary method of dealing with "one thing at a time" we may first proceed to abolish the Lords' veto, we cannot halt there. That change, as we perceive, will not leave other things as they were, but will demand a thorough-going many-sided reconstruction of our representative system, unless we wish to abandon the cause of political self-government.

Several reforms are needed, besides the destruction of the Lords' veto, in order to convert the present representative system into an effective instrument of democracy. The House of Commons must be made more accurately representative, and representative government must be supplemented by a measure of direct democratic control. In order to make the House of Commons representative of the will of the people, it must be in direct and frequent contact with the needs, aspirations, and experience of the whole people. Though capacity to serve the State is the true basis of the suffrage, and this capacity must be greater in some citizens than in others, no safe method of enforcing this theoretically justifiable discrimination is discoverable. Adult suffrage is the only practicable expedient for securing the required contact between representatives and people. In every country where democracy has taken root the basis of representation has broadened towards this shape. The admission of women to an equal voice with men thus needs no separate argument. It inheres in the very nature of democracy. For a democracy maimed by the exclusion of the direct representation of the needs, aspirations, and experience of half the people would be a mere androcracy.

With the same object of rendering the House of Commons a truer expression of the popular will, some form of proportional representation must be incorporated in our electoral system. Three definite evils are traceable to the defective working of the present system. First, there is the party majority in the House of Commons exaggerated beyond all proper proportion to the aggregate electoral majority in the country, and lending itself, as we have seen, to Cabinet autocracy. Secondly, there is the abuse of pledges imposed upon candidates by minorities which, under proportional representation with fairly large areas, would spend their electoral strength upon electing a few zealous supporters of their special causes. Thirdly, there is the loss to the State of many of her ablest and most honourable legislators who cannot hope or desire to obtain election under the existing system of polling. The single transferable vote, applied in areas of sufficient size to enable every considerable minority to be represented, is so simple and so manifestly just a reform that it could not fail to win popular acceptance, if a fair opportunity were secured for the recasting of our electoral machinery.

If to these major reforms we added the destruction of the present plural vote and the payment of members and electoral expenses out of public funds, we should have secured the forms of sound representation. But two democratic requirements would still remain unfulfilled. Though proportional representation would mitigate the tyranny of majority rule, and would curb to some extent the autocracy of Governments, astute party management or personal ambition might generate new abuses such as attend the play of the group system in some continental legislatures. Moreover, it is unlikely that the reforms of electoral institutions, here proposed, would of themselves so strengthen the House of Commons as to reverse the tendency towards increased Cabinet control. A real and firm check upon abuse of power on the part of a Cabinet and a House of Commons called upon to deal with new and urgent issues upon which the electorate had not been consulted, is an essential of democracy. Nor are such the only occasions which require a check. Elected legislators, mostly amateurs, will of necessity be influenced strongly, sometimes predominantly, by those able permanent officials who, in the intricate processes of modern government, must necessarily come to play a growing part in the construction and administration of laws. Now this official mind, eminently serviceable, has its inevitable defects; authoritative, excessively conservative, mechanical, and usually contemptuous of the lay civic mind, it is apt to use every opportunity to impose itself upon new legislative proposals, and to substitute, as far as possible, the official will for the representative will. Now, though in nine cases out of ten this co-operation of the skilled official may be highly beneficial, there will be certain cases where his determinant influence will definitely conflict with the wisdom of the will of the people. This is no matter of mere theory. The fact cannot be blinked that, for some time to come, high officials in this country will, by their economic interests, their upbringing, and their social habits, be in most imperfect sympathy with the aspirations of democracy. Consciously, or more often unconsciously, these class sentiments or interests will obtrude themselves into the advisory and formative work of legislation and administration which falls to them. How should it be otherwise? Until a far fuller measure of equality of economic and intellectual opportunity exists than now, a powerful support must continue to be rendered by the higher bureaucracy to the defence of vested interests upon the political field.

The only effective check upon these defects or abuses of representative government is a direct appeal to the people. This Referendum is based upon a recognition that no form of representation is perfect, and that certain particular defects in representative government can best be met by a special and direct appeal to the fount of government. The will or consent of the people is in fact always claimed on behalf of every important measure of our legislature. But there exists no means of testing this claim. Electoral pledges, or post-electoral resolutions of caucuses or of other gatherings of electors, are, as we have seen, ineffective and often injurious methods of conveying a mandate or a consent. But the growing part they play in politics must be interpreted as an instinctive endeavour of the popular will to express particular judgments and to supplement the purely representative principle by some closer and more intimate control.

Part 2

CAMPAIGNS AND GROUPS

8

SOCIETY FOR CONSTITUTIONAL INFORMATION

Source: Society for Constitutional Information, 1783, pp. i–ii

THE design of this Society is to diffuse throughout the kingdom, as universally as possible, a knowledge of the great principles of Constitutional Freedom, particularly such as respect the election and duration of the representative body. With this view Constitutional Tracts, intended for the extension of this knowledge, and to communicate it to persons of all ranks, are printed and distributed GRATIS, at the expence of the Society. Essays, and extracts from various authors, calculated to promote the same design, are also published under the direction of the Society, in several of the News-papers: and it is the wish of the Society to extend this knowledge throughout every part of the united kingdoms, and to convince men of all ranks, that it is their interest, as well as their duty, to support a free constitution, and to maintain and assert those common rights, which are essential to the dignity, and to the happiness of human nature.

To procure short parliaments, and a more equal representation of the people, are the primary objects of the attention of this Society, and they wish to disseminate that knowledge among their Countrymen, which may lead them to a general sense of the importance of these objects, and which may induce them to contend for their rights, as men, and as citizens, with ardour and with firmness.

The communication of sound political knowledge to the people at large must be of great national advantage; as nothing but ignorance of their natural rights, or inattention to the consequence of those rights to their interest and happiness, can induce the majority of the inhabitants of any country to submit to any species of civil tyranny. Public Freedom is the source of national dignity, and of national felicity; and it is the duty of every friend to virtue and mankind to exert himself in the promotion of it.

9
THE LONDON CORRESPONDING SOCIETY'S REGULATIONS

Source: London Corresponding Society, 24 May 1792

ASSURED that Man, individual Man, may justly claim LIBERTY as his birthright, we naturally conclude, that, as a Member of Society, it becomes his indispensible duty to preserve inviolate that liberty for the benefit of his Fellow Citizens, and of his and their Prosperity.

For, as in the associating, he gave up certain of his Rights in order to secure the possession of the remainder, and VOLUNTARILY yielded up only as much as was necessary for the general good, for he may not barter away the Liberties of his prosperity for the general good, nor defeat the common cause by TAMELY and SUPINELY suffering to be purloined from the People, of whom he makes a part, their natural and unalienable RIGHTS OF RESISTANCE to OPPRESSION, and of SHARING IN THE GOVERNMENT OF THEIR COUNTRY; without the full and uninterrupted exercise of which RIGHTS, no man can with truth call himself or his country free.

Yet of late, the very men who have dared to oppress the nation, have also dared to advance, that – all RESISTANCE TO THEIR OPPRESSION IS ILLEGAL: – while on the other hand, FRAUD and FORCE, sanctioned by Custom and blind Submission, has withdrawn, and now withholds, from a very great majority of the Tax-paying, industrious and useful inhabitants of Great Britain, the RIGHT of sharing in the Governing of their own Commonwealth, and in the management of THEIR own Interests.

The few who are permitted to elect Representatives, and those who are chosen by this SMALL NUMBER OF ELECTORS, disgrace the Country at large, by BUYING and SELLING Votes, by CORRUPTING, or being CORRUPTED – the former by their behaviour at Elections, and the latter by their conduct in the Senate – more than sufficient to prove that THE NATION IS UNREPRESENTED, and that THE PRESENT SYSTEM IS TOTALLY INCONSTITUTIONAL – if by the word Constitution any thing is meant.

Roused at last from their Torpor, and eager to remedy the evil – various, numerous, and respectable Societies have been formed by the people, in different parts of the Kingdom; several have also arisen in the Metropolis; and among them

The London Corresponding Society,

with modesty, but firmness, claim the attention of their Country to the following Resolved

RESOLUTIONS

I. That every Individual has a RIGHT to share in the Government of that Society of which he is a Member – unless incapacitated.
II. That nothing but Non-age, privation of Reason, or an offence against the general Laws of Society, can Incapacitate him.
III. That it is no less the Right than the Duty of every Citizen to keep a watchful Eye on the Governance of his Country, that the Law, by being multiplied, do not degenerate into Oppression: and that those who are intrusted with the Government, do not substitute PRIVATE INTEREST for PUBLIC ADVANTAGE.
IV. That the People of Great Britain are not EFFECTUALLY represented in Parliament.
V. That, in consequence of a partial, unequal, and therefore INADEQUATE REPRESENTATION, together with the CORRUPT method in which the Representatives are Elected; Oppressive Taxes, Unjust Laws, Restrictions of Liberty, and wasting of Public Money, have ensued.
VI. That the only Remedy to these Evils is a fair, equal, and impartial Representation of the People in Parliament.
VII. That a fair, equal and impartial Representation can never take place till all PARTIAL PRIVILEGES ARE ABOLISHED.
VIII. That THIS SOCIETY do express their abhorrence to Tumult and Violence; aiming to REFORM, not ANARCHY – Reason, Firmness, and Unanimity, are the only Arms they themselves will employ, or persuade their fellow Citizens to exert, AGAINST ABUSE OF POWER.

Signed, by Order of the Committee,
M. MARGAROT, CHAIRMAN,
T, HARDY, SECRETARY

WHEREAS it is notorious that very numerous, burthensome, and unnecessary Taxes are laid on the Persons and families of us, and others, the Industrious Inhabitants of Great Britain, an exceedingly great Majority of whom are, notwithstanding, excluded from all Representation in Parliament.

And as upon inquiry into th Cause of this GRIEVANCE, which is at once a reflection of our industry, and a diminution of our Property, we hold that the Constitution of our Country (which was purchased for us, AT THE EXPENCE OF THE LIVES OF OUR ANCESTORS) has, by the Violence and Intrigue of criminal and designing Men, been injured and undermined n its most essential and important parts; but particularly in the House of Commons, where the whole of te supposed Representation of the People is neither more nor less than an Usurped Power, arising either from Abuses in the mode of Election and Duration of Parliaments, or from a Corrupt Property in certain Decayed Corporations, by means of which the Liberties of this Nation are basely bartered away for private profit of Members of Parliament.

And as it further appears to us that, until this Source of Corruption shall be cleansed by the Information, Perseverance, Firmness, and Union of the People at large, we are robbed of the inheritance so acquired for us by our forefathers; and that our Taxes, instead of being lessened, will go on increasing; inasmuch as they will furnish Bribes, Places, and Pensions, to our Ministers and Members of Parliament.

It being resolved by us, the Members of this Society to unite ourselves into one firm and permanent Body, for the purpose of informing ourselves and others of the exact State of the present PARLIAMENTARY Representation: – For obtaining a Peaceful but Adequate Remedy to this intolerable grievance – and for corresponding and co-operating with other Societies, united for the same objects: The following

REGULATIONS

For the internal order and government of our Society have been adopted.

10

'MASQUE OF ANARCHY'

Percy Bysshe Shelley

Source: 'Masque of Anarchy', 1819

1

As I lay asleep in Italy
There came a voice from over the Sea,
And with great power it forth led me
To walk in the visions of Poesy.

2

I met Murder on the way –
He had a mask like Castlereagh –
Very smooth he looked, yet grim;
Seven blood-hounds followed him:

3

All were fat; and well they might
Be in admirable plight, 10
For one by one, and two by two,
He tossed them human hearts to chew

4

Which from his wide cloak he drew.
Next came Fraud, and he had on,
Like Eldon, an ermined gown;
His big tears, for he wept well,
Turned to mill-stones as they fell.

5

And the little children, who
Round his feet played to and fro,

Thinking every tear a gem, 20
Had their brains knocked out by them.

6

Clothed with the Bible, as with light,
And the shadows of the night,
Like Sidmouth, next, Hypocrisy
On a crocodile rode by.

7

And many more Destructions played
In this ghastly masquerade,
All disguised, even to the eyes,
Like Bishops, lawyers, peers, or spies.

8

Last came Anarchy: he rode 30
On a white horse, splashed with blood;
He was pale even to the lips,
Like Death in the Apocalypse.

9

And he wore a kingly crown;
And in his grasp a sceptre shone;
On his brow this mark I saw –
'I AM GOD, AND KING, AND LAW!'

10

With a pace stately and fast,
Over English land he passed,
Trampling to a mire of blood 40
The adoring multitude.

11

And a mighty troop around,
With their trampling shook the ground,
Waving each a bloody sword,
For the service of their Lord.

12

And with glorious triumph, they
Rode through England proud and gay,
Drunk as with intoxication
Of the wine of desolation.

13

O'er fields and towns, from sea to sea, 50
Passed the Pageant swift and free,
Tearing up, and trampling down;
Till they came to London town.

14

And each dweller, panic-stricken,
Felt his heart with terror sicken
Hearing the tempestuous cry
Of the triumph of Anarchy.

15

For with pomp to meet him came,
Clothed in arms like blood and flame,
The hired murderers, who did sing 60
'Thou art God, and Law, and King.

16

We have waited, weak and lone
For thy coming, Mighty One!
Our purses are empty, our swords are cold,
Give us glory, and blood, and gold.'

17

Lawyers and priests, a motley crowd,
To the earth their pale brows bowed;
Like a bad prayer not over loud,
Whispering – 'Thou art Law and God.' –

18

Then all cried with one accord, 70
'Thou art King, and God, and Lord;

Anarchy, to thee we bow,
Be thy name made holy now!'

19

And Anarchy, the Skeleton,
Bowed and grinned to every one,
As well as if his education
Had cost ten millions to the nation.

20

For he knew the Palaces
Of our Kings were rightly his;
His the sceptre, crown, and globe, 80
And the gold-inwoven robe.

21

So he sent his slaves before
To seize upon the Bank and Tower,
And was proceeding with intent
To meet his pensioned Parliament

22

When one fled past, a maniac maid,
And her name was Hope, she said:
But she looked more like Despair,
And she cried out in the air:

23

'My father Time is weak and gray 90
With waiting for a better day;
See how idiot-like he stands,
Fumbling with his palsied hands!

24

'He has had child after child,
And the dust of death is piled
Over every one but me –
Misery, oh, Misery!'

25

Then she lay down in the street,
Right before the horses' feet,
Expecting, with a patient eye, 100
Murder, Fraud, and Anarchy.

26

When between her and her foes
A mist, a light, an image rose,
Small at first, and weak, and frail
Like the vapour of a vale:

27

Till as clouds grow on the blast,
Like tower-crowned giants striding fast,
And glare with lightnings as they fly,
And speak in thunder to the sky,

28

It grew – a Shape arrayed in mail 110
Brighter than the viper's scale,
And upborne on wings whose grain
Was as the light of sunny rain.

29

On its helm, seen far away,
A planet, like the Morning's, lay;
And those plumes its light rained through
Like a shower of crimson dew.

30

With step as soft as wind it passed
O'er the heads of men – so fast
That they knew the presence there, 120
And looked, – but all was empty air.

31

As flowers beneath May's footstep waken,
As stars from Night's loose hair are shaken,

As waves arise when loud winds call,
Thoughts sprung where'er that step did fall.

32

And the prostrate multitude
Looked – and ankle-deep in blood,
Hope, that maiden most serene,
Was walking with a quiet mien:

33

And Anarchy, the ghastly birth, 130
Lay dead earth upon the earth;
The Horse of Death tameless as wind
Fled, and with his hoofs did grind
To dust the murderers thronged behind.

34

A rushing light of clouds and splendour,
A sense awakening and yet tender
Was heard and felt – and at its close
These words of joy and fear arose

35

As if their own indignant Earth
Which gave the sons of England birth 140
Had felt their blood upon her brow,
And shuddering with a mother's throe

36

Had turnèd every drop of blood
By which her face had been bedewed
To an accent unwithstood,–
As if her heart had cried aloud:

37

'Men of England, heirs of Glory,
Heroes of unwritten story,
Nurslings of one mighty Mother,
Hopes of her, and one another; 150

38

'Rise like Lions after slumber
In unvanquishable number,
Shake your chains to earth like dew
Which in sleep had fallen on you –
Ye are many – they are few.

39

'What is Freedom? – ye can tell
That which slavery is, too well –
For its very name has grown
To an echo of your own.<

40

'Tis to work and have such pay 160
As just keeps life from day to day
In your limbs, as in a cell
For the tyrants' use to dwell,

41

'So that ye for them are made
Loom, and plough, and sword, and spade,
With or without your own will bent
To their defence and nourishment.

42

'Tis to see your children weak
With their mothers pine and peak,
When the winter winds are bleak,– 170
They are dying whilst I speak.

43

'Tis to hunger for such diet
As the rich man in his riot
Casts to the fat dogs that lie
Surfeiting beneath his eye;

44

'Tis to let the Ghost of Gold
Take from Toil a thousandfold

45

'Paper coin – that forgery 180
Of the title-deeds, which ye
Hold to something of the worth
Of the inheritance of Earth.

46

'Tis to be a slave in soul
And to hold no strong control
Over your own wills, but be
All that others make of ye.

47

'And at length when ye complain
With a murmur weak and vain
'Tis to see the Tyrant's crew 190
Ride over your wives and you –
Blood is on the grass like dew.

48

'Then it is to feel revenge
Fiercely thirsting to exchange
Blood for blood – and wrong for wrong –
Do not thus when ye are strong.

49

'Birds find rest, in narrow nest
When weary of their wingèd quest;
Beasts find fare, in woody lair
When storm and snow are in the air, 200

50

'Asses, swine, have litter spread
And with fitting food are fed;
All things have a home but one –
Thou, Oh, Englishman, hast none!

51

'This is Slavery – savage men,
Or wild beasts within a den
Would endure not as ye do –
But such ills they never knew.

52

'What art thou Freedom? O! could slaves
Answer from their living graves 210
This demand – tyrants would flee
Like a dream's dim imagery:

53

'Thou art not, as impostors say,
A shadow soon to pass away,
A superstition, and a name
Echoing from the cave of Fame.

54

'For the labourer thou art bread,
And a comely table spread
From his daily labour come
In a neat and happy home. 220

55

'Thou art clothes, and fire, and food
For the trampled multitude –
No – in countries that are free
Such starvation cannot be
As in England now we see.

56

'To the rich thou art a check,
When his foot is on the neck
Of his victim, thou dost make
That he treads upon a snake.

57

'Thou art Justice – ne'er for gold 230
May thy righteous laws be sold

58

'Thou art Wisdom – Freemen never
Dream that God will damn for ever
All who think those things untrue
Of which Priests make such ado.

59

'Thou art Peace – never by thee
Would blood and treasure wasted be
As tyrants wasted them, when all
Leagued to quench thy flame in Gaul.

60

'What if English toil and blood
Was poured forth, even as a flood?
It availed, Oh, Liberty,
To dim, but not extinguish thee.

61

'Thou art Love – the rich have kissed
Thy feet, and like him following Christ,
Give their substance to the free
And through the rough world follow thee,

62

'Or turn their wealth to arms, and make
War for thy belovèd sake
On wealth, and war, and fraud – whence they
Drew the power which is their prey.

63

'Science, Poetry, and Thought
Are thy lamps; they make the lot
Of the dwellers in a cot
So serene, they curse it not.

64

'Spirit, Patience, Gentleness,
All that can adorn and bless
Art thou – let deeds, not words, express 260
Thine exceeding loveliness.

65

'Let a great Assembly be
Of the fearless and the free
On some spot of English ground
Where the plains stretch wide around.

66

'Let the blue sky overhead,
The green earth on which ye tread,
All that must eternal be
Witness the solemnity.

67

'From the corners uttermost 270
Of the bonds of English coast;
From every hut, village, and town
Where those who live and suffer moan
For others' misery or their own.

68

'From the workhouse and the prison
Where pale as corpses newly risen,
Women, children, young and old
Groan for pain, and weep for cold –

69

'From the haunts of daily life
Where is waged the daily strife 280
With common wants and common cares
Which sows the human heart with tares –

70

'Lastly from the palaces
Where the murmur of distress

Echoes, like the distant sound
Of a wind alive around

71

'Those prison halls of wealth and fashion,
Where some few feel such compassion
For those who groan, and toil, and wail
As must make their brethren pale – 290

72

'Ye who suffer woes untold,
Or to feel, or to behold
Your lost country bought and sold
With a price of blood and gold –

73

'Let a vast assembly be,
And with great solemnity
Declare with measured words that ye
Are, as God has made ye, free –

74

'Be your strong and simple words
Keen to wound as sharpened swords, 300
And wide as targes let them be,
With their shade to cover ye.

75

'Let the tyrants pour around
With a quick and startling sound,
Like the loosening of a sea,
Troops of armed emblazonry.

76

'Let the charged artillery drive
Till the dead air seems alive
With the clash of clanging wheels,
And the tramp of horses' heels. 310

77

'Let the fixèd bayonet
Gleam with sharp desire to wet
Its bright point in English blood
Looking keen as one for food.

78

'Let the horsemen's scimitars
Wheel and flash, like sphereless stars
Thirsting to eclipse their burning
In a sea of death and mourning.

79

'Stand ye calm and resolute,
Like a forest close and mute, 320
With folded arms and looks which are
Weapons of unvanquished war,

80

'And let Panic, who outspeeds
The career of armèd steeds
Pass, a disregarded shade
Through your phalanx undismayed.

81

'Let the laws of your own land,
Good or ill, between ye stand
Hand to hand, and foot to foot,
Arbiters of the dispute, 330

82

'The old laws of England – they
Whose reverend heads with age are gray,
Children of a wiser day;
And whose solemn voice must be
Thine own echo – Liberty!

83

'On those who first should violate
Such sacred heralds in their state

84

'And if then the tyrants dare 340
Let them ride among you there,
Slash, and stab, and maim, and hew,–
What they like, that let them do.

85

'With folded arms and steady eyes,
And little fear, and less surprise,
Look upon them as they slay
Till their rage has died away.

86

'Then they will return with shame
To the place from which they came,
And the blood thus shed will speak 350
In hot blushes on their cheek.

87

'Every woman in the land
Will point at them as they stand –
They will hardly dare to greet
Their acquaintance in the street.

88

'And the bold, true warriors
Who have hugged Danger in wars
Will turn to those who would be free,
Ashamed of such base company.

89

'And that slaughter to the Nation 360
Shall steam up like inspiration,
Eloquent, oracular;
A volcano heard afar.

90

'And these words shall then become
Like Oppression's thundered doom
Ringing through each heart and brain,
Heard again – again – again –

91

'Rise like Lions after slumber
In unvanquishable number –
Shake your chains to earth like dew 370
Which in sleep had fallen on you –
Ye are many – they are few.'

11

'THE PEOPLE'S CHARTER – PETITION'

Thomas Duncombe

Source: House of Commons, 2 May 1842

[A Petition from the working classes throughout the kingdom, of the presentation of which Mr. Thomas Duncombe had previously given notice, was brought down to the House, by a procession consisting of a vast multitude. Its bulk was so great, that the doors were not wide enough to admit it, and it was necessary to unrol it, to carry it into the House. When unrolled, it spread over a great part of the floor, and rose above the level of the Table.]

Mr. T. Duncombe, in presenting it to the House, said, – Looking at the vast proportions of this petition – looking, too, at the importance attaching to it, not only from the matter it contains, but from the millions who have signed it, I am quite satisfied, that if I were to ask the House to relax the rules which it has laid down to govern the presentation of petitions, it would grant me the indulgence; but as I have given notice of a motion for to-morrow, that the petition should be taken into the serious consideration of the House, and that those who have signed it, should by their counsel and agents, be heard at the Bar of your House, in support of the allegations which the petition contains, I shall not ask the House to grant me that indulgence, but will keep myself strictly within the limits which have been laid down for the presentation of all petitions. I beg respectfully to offer to the acceptance of this House, a petition signed by 3,315,752 of the industrious classes of this country. The petition proceeds from those upon whose toil, upon whose industry, upon whose affection, and upon whose attachment, I may say, every institution, every law, nay, even the very Government, and the whole property and commerce of the country depend. These persons now most respectfully come before you, to state the manifold grievances under which they are suffering. They state those grievances at some length; I need not now go through them, because I mean to ask your Clerk to read them at the Table. I may state, however, that they attribute the manifold grievances and distresses, which they are now enduring, and have for a considerable length of time endured, to class-legislation and to the misrepresentation of their interests in this House. They state, that for a considerable length of time their interests have been grossly neglected, and that no interests beyond your own, have ever been thought of "within your walls." They are ready to prove this at your Bar. In the first place, they ask you to hear them. They state in their prayer: – That they cannot within the limits of this their petition, set forth even a tithe of the many grievances of which they may justly complain; but should your honourable House be pleased to grant your petitioners a hearing, by representatives at the Bar of your honourable House, your petitioners will be enabled to unfold a tale of wrong and suffering – of intolerable injustice – which will create utter astonishment in the minds of all benevolent and good men, that the people of Great Britain and Ireland, have so long quietly endured their wretched condition, brought upon them, as it has been, by unjust exclusion from political authority, and by the manifold corruptions of class legislation. This petition proceeds, as I have stated, from 3,315,752 of the industrious classes. I have in my hand, a short analysis of the places in which the greater number of the signatures to the petition were obtained. The list of hamlets and towns from which less than 10,000 signatures were procured, is so very long, that I will not detain the House by reading it. I will name those towns only from which more than 10,000 have been obtained. They are these: Manchester, 99,680; Newcastle and districts, 92,000; Glasgow and Lanarkshire, 78,062; Halifax, 36,400; Nottingham, 40,000; Leeds, 41,000; Birmingham, 43,000; Norwich, 21,560; Bolton, 18,500; Leicester, 18,000; Rochdale, 19,600; Loughborough and districts, 10,000; Sal-ford, 19,600; East Riding, Yorkshire, agricultural districts, 14,840; Worcester, 10,000; Merthyr Tydvil and districts, 13,900; Aberdeen, 17,600; Keithly, 11,000; Brighton, 12,700; Bristol, 12,800; Huddersfield, 23,180; Sheffield, 27,200; Scotland, West Midland districts, 18,000; Dunfermline, 16,000; Cheltenham, 10,400; Liverpool, 23,000; Staley. bridge and districts, 10,000; Stockport, 14,000; Macclesfield and suburbs, 10,000; North Lancashire, 52,000; Oldham, 15,000; Ashton, 14,200; Bradford and district, Yorkshire, 45,100; Burnley, and district, 14,000; Preston and district, 24,000; Wigan, 10,000; London and suburbs, 200,000; from 371 other towns, villages, &c.2,154,807 – Total, 3,315,752. I believe these to be every one of them bonâ fide signatures. The remedies that the petitioners suggest would be that they should have a voice in the election of representatives; that they should be represented in this House. They complain that at present they are totally and grossly misrepresented; and they pray that, after having heard them, if you should be satisfied with their arguments, you do immediately, without alteration, deduction, or addition, pass into a law the document entitled "The People's Charter;" which embraces the representation of male adults, vote by ballot, annual Parliaments, no property qualification, payment of members, and equal electoral districts. And your petitioners, desiring to promote the peace of the United Kingdom, security of property, and prosperity of commerce, seriously and earnestly press this their petition on the attention of your honourable House. I beg leave to move that this petition be brought up and read by the Clerk at the Table.

The petition was read by the Clerk, as follows: – TO THE HONOURABLE THE COMMONS OF GREAT BRITAIN AND IRELAND, IN PARLIAMENT ASSEMBLED. The petition of the undersigned people of the United Kingdom,

Sheweth – That Government originated from, was designed to protect the freedom and promote the happiness of, and ought to be responsible to, the whole people. That the only authority on which any body of men can make laws and govern society, is delegation from the people. That as Government was designed for the benefit and protection of, and must be obeyed and supported by all, therefore all should be equally represented. That any form of Government which fails to effect the purposes for which it was designed, and does not fully and completely represent the whole people, who are compelled to pay taxes to its support and obey the laws resolved upon by it, is unconstitutional, tyrannical, and ought to be amended or resisted. That your honourable House, as at present constituted, has not been elected by, and acts irresponsibly of, the people; and hitherto has only represented parties, and benefitted the few, regardless of the miseries, grievances, and petitions of the many. Your honourable House has enacted laws contrary to the expressed wishes of the people, and by unconstitutional means enforced obedience to them, thereby creating an unbearable despotism on the one hand, and degrading slavery on the other. That if your honourable House is of opinion that the people of Great Britain and Ireland ought not to be fully represented, your petitioners pray that such opinion may be unequivocally made known, that the people may fully understand what they can or cannot expect from your honourable House; because if such be the decision of your honourable House, your petitioners are of opinion that where representation is denied, taxation ought to be resisted. That your petitioners instance, in proof of their assertion, that your honourable House has not been elected by the people; that the population of Great Britain and Ireland is at the present time about twenty-six millions of persons; and that yet, out of this number, little more than nine hundred thousand have been permitted to vote in the recent election of representatives to make laws to govern the whole. That the existing state of representation is not only extremely limited and unjust, but unequally divided, and gives preponderating influence to the landed and monied interests, to the utter ruin of the small-trading and labouring classes. That the borough of Guilford, with a population of 3,920 returns to Parliament as many members as the Tower Hamlets, with a population of 300,000; Evesham, with a population of 3,998, elects as many representatives as Manchester, with a population of 200,000; and Buckingham, Evesham, Totness, Guildford, Honiton, and Bridport, with a total population of 23,000, return as many representatives as Manchester, Finsbury, Tower Hamlets, Liverpool, Marylebone, and Lambeth, with a population of 1,400,000! these being but a very few instances of the enormous inequalities existing in what is called the representation of this country. That bribery, intimidation, corruption, perjury, and riot, prevail at all parliamentary elections, to an extent best understood by the Members of your honourable House. That your petitioners complain that they are enormously taxed to pay the interest of what is termed the national debt, a debt amounting at present to 800,000,000l., being only a portion of the enormous amount expended in cruel and expensive wars for the suppression of all liberty, by men not authorised by the people, and who, consequently, had no right to tax posterity for the outrages committed by them upon mankind. And your petitioners loudly complain of the augmentation of that debt, after twenty-six years of almost uninterrupted peace, and whilst poverty and discontent rage over the land. That taxation, both general and local, is at this time too enormous to be borne; and in the opinion of your petitioners is contrary to the spirit of the Bill of Rights, wherein it is clearly expressed that no subject shall be compelled to contribute to any tax, talliage, or aid, unless imposed by common consent in Parliament. That in England, Ireland, Scotland, and Wales, thousands of people are dying from actual want; and your petitioners, whilst sensible that poverty is the great exciting cause of crime, view with mingled astonishment and alarm the ill provision made for the poor, the aged, and infirm; and likewise perceive, with feelings of indignation, the determination of your honourable House to continue the Poor-law Bill in operation, notwithstanding the many proofs which have been afforded by sad experience of the unconstitutional principal of that bill, of its unchristian character, and of the cruel and murderous effects produced upon the wages of working men, and the lives of the subjects of this realm. That your petitioners conceive that bill to be contrary to all previous statutes, opposed to the spirit of the constitution, and an actual violation of the precepts of the Christian religion; and, therefore, your petitioners look with apprehension to the results which may flow from its continuance. That your petitioners would direct the attention of your honourable House to the great disparity existing between the wages of the producing millions, and the salaries of those whose comparative usefulness ought to be questioned, where riches and luxury prevail amongst the rulers, and poverty and starvation amongst the ruled. That your petitioners, with all due respect and loyalty, would compare the daily income of the Sovereign Majesty with that of thousands of the working men of this nation; and whilst your petitioners have learned that her Majesty receives daily for her private use the sum of 164l. 17s. 10d., they have also ascertained that many thousands of the families of the labourers are only in the receipt of 3¾d. per head per day. That your petitioners have also learned that his royal Highness Prince Albert receives each day the sum of 104l. 2s., whilst thousands have to exist upon 3d. per head per day. That your petitioners have also heard with astonishment, that the King of Hanover daily receives 57l. 10s. whilst thousands of the tax-payers of this empire live upon 2¾d. per head per day. That your petitioners have, with pain and regret, also learned that the Archbishop of Canterbury is daily in the receipt of 52l. 10s. per day, whilst thousands of the poor have to maintain their families upon an income not exceeding 2d. per head per day. That notwithstanding the wretched and unparalleled condition of the people, your honourable House has manifested no disposition to curtail the expenses of the State, to diminish taxation, or promote general prosperity. That unless immediate remedial measures be adopted, your petitioners fear the increasing distress of the people will lead to results fearful to contemplate; because your petitioners can produce evidence of the gradual decline of wages, at the same time that the constant increase of the national burdens must be apparent to all. That your petitioners know that it is the undoubted constitutional right of the people, to meet freely, when, how, and where they choose, in public places, peaceably, in the day, to discuss their grievances, and political or other subjects, or for the purpose of framing discussing, or passing any vote, petition, or remonstrance, upon any subject whatsoever. That your petitioners complain that the right has unconstitutionally been infringed; and 500 well disposed persons have been arrested, excessive bail demanded, tried by packed juries, sentenced to imprisonment, and treated as felons of the worst description. That an unconstitutional police force is distributed all over the country, at enormous cost, to prevent the due exercise of the people's rights. And your petitioners are of opinion that the Poor-law Bastiles and the police stations, being co-existent, have originated from the same cause, viz., the increased desire on the part of the irresponsible few to oppress and starve the many. That a vast and unconstitutional army is upheld at the public expense, for the purpose of repressing public opinion in the three kingdoms, and likewise to intimidate the millions in the due exercise of those rights and privileges which ought to belong to them. That your petitioners complain that the hours of labour, particularly of the factory workers, are protracted beyond the limits of human endurance, and that the wages earned, after unnatural application to toil in heated and unhealthy workshops, are inadequate to sustain the bodily strength, and supply those comforts which are so imperative after an excessive waste of physical energy. That your petitioners also direct the attention of your honourable House to the starvation wages of the agricultural labourer, and view with horror and indignation the paltry income of those whose toil gives being to the staple food of this people. That your petitioners, deeply deplore the existence of any kind of monopoly in this nation, and whilst they unequivocally condemn the levying of any tax upon the necessaries of life, and upon those articles principally required by the labouring classes, they are also sensible that the abolition of any one monopoly will never unshackle labour from its misery until the people possess that power under which all monopoly and oppression must cease; and your petitioners respectfully mention the existing monopolies of the suffrage, of paper money, of machinery, of land, of the public press, of religious privileges, of the means of travelling and transit, and a host of other evils too numerous to mention, all arising from class legislation, but which your honourable House has always consistently endeavoured to increase instead of diminish. That your petitioners are sensible, from the numerous petitions presented to your honourable House, that your honourable House is fully acquainted with the grievances of the working men; and your petitioners pray that the rights and wrongs of labour may be considered, with a view to the protection of the one, and to the removal of the other; because your petitioners are of opinion that it is the worst species of legislation which leaves the grievances of society to be removed only by violence or revolution, both of which may be apprehended if complaints are unattended to and petitions despised. That your petitioners complain that upwards of nine millions of pounds per annum are unjustly abstracted from them to maintain a church establishment, from which they principally dissent; and beg to Call the attention of your honourable House to the fact, that this enormous sum is equal to, if it does not exceed, the cost of upholding Christianity in all parts of the world beside. Your petitioners complain that it is unjust, and not in accordance with the Christian religion, to enforce compulsory support of religious creeds, and expensive church establishments, with which the people do not agree. That your petitioners believe all men have a right to worship God as may appear best to their consciences, and that no legislative enactments should interfere between man and his Creator. That your petitioners direct the attention of your honourable House to the enormous revenue annually swallowed up by the bishops and the clergy, and entreat you to contrast their deeds with the conduct of the founder of the Christian religion, who denounced worshippers of Mammon, and taught charity, meekness, and brotherly love. That your petitioners strongly complain that the people of this kingdom are subject to the rule of irresponsible lawmakers, to whom they have given no authority, and are enormously taxed to uphold a corrupt system, to which they have never in person or by representation given their assent. That your petitioners maintain that it is the inherent, indubitable, and constitutional right, founded upon the ancient practice of the realm of England, and supported by well approved statutes, of every male inhabitant of the United Kingdom, he being of age and of sound mind, non-convict of crime, and not confined under any judicial process, to exercise the elective franchise in the choice of Members to serve in the Commons House of Parliament. That your petitioners can prove, that by the ancient customs and statutes of this realm, Parliament should be held once in each year. That your petitioners maintain that Members elected to serve in Parliament ought to be the servants of the people, and should, at short and stated intervals, return to their constituencies, to ascertain if their conduct is approved of, and to give the people power to reject all who have not acted honestly and justly. That your petitioners complain that possession of property is made the test of men's qualification to sit in Parliament. That your petitioners can give proof that such qualification is irrational, unnecessary, and not in accordance with the ancient usages of England. That your petitioners complain, that by influence, patronage, and intimidation, there is at present no purity of election; and your petitioners contend for the right of voting by ballot. That your petitioners complain that seats in your honourable House are sought for at a most extravagant rate of expense; which proves an enormous degree of fraud and corruption. That your petitioners, therefore, contend, that to put an end to secret political traffic, all representatives should be paid a limited amount for their services. That your petitioners complain of the inequality of representation; and contend for the division of the country into equal electoral districts. That your petitioners complain of the many grievances borne by the people of Ireland, and contend that they are fully entitled to a repeal of the legislative union. That your petitioners have viewed with great indignation the partiality shown to the aristocracy in the courts of justice, and the cruelty of that system of law which deprived Frost, Williams, and Jones, of the benefit of the objection offered by Sir Frederick Pollock during the trial at Monmouth, and which was approved of by a large majority of the judges. That your petitioners beg to assure your honourable House that they cannot, within the limits of this their petition, set forth even a tithe of the many grievances of which they may justly complain; but should your honourable House be pleased to grant your petitioners a hearing by representatives at the Bar of your honourable House, your petitioners will be enabled to unfold a tale of wrong and suffering – of intolerable injustice – which will create utter astonishment in the minds of all benevolent and good men, that the people of Great Britain and Ireland have so long quietly endured their wretched condition, brought upon them as it has been by unjust exclusion from political authority, and by the manifold corruptions of class-legislation. That your petitioners, therefore, exercising their just constitutional right, demand that your honourable House do remedy the many gross and manifest evils of which your petitioners complain, do immediately, without alteration, deduction, or addition, pass into a law the document entitled 'The People's Charter,' which embraces the representation of male adults, vote by ballot, annual Parliaments, no property qualification, payment of Members, and equal electoral districts. And that your petitioners, desiring to promote the peace of the United Kingdom, security of property, and prosperity of commerce, seriously and earnestly press this, their petition, on the attention of your honourable House. And your petitioners, &c. Petition to be printed.

12

ADDRESS OF THE COMMITTEE TO THE PEOPLE OF ENGLAND

Source: Administrative Reform Association, 19 May 1855

There must be an end put to every mystery of office – how the Administration of the country is carried on must be made plain to the most ordinary capacity. To this end Acts of Parliament must be searched – and returns obtained. The Association are resolved to have a complete Analysis of our Official System, a thorough clearing up of the question of personal responsibility. This will, of necessity, be a work of time and expense; the Committee, however, are perfectly satisfied that the required means will be forthcoming, that subscriptions to the object will be general throughout the country, that a failing purse will never compel them to hold their hand. They have already entered upon this portion of their labour, with the most experienced and energetic help, and will shortly be able to place some valuable information, in a convenient form, in the hands of the Members of the Association. A knowledge of the actual state of the official system once attained, the next step will be to bring every department into a thoroughly business condition. The nation can afford to pension, even upon full pay, any amount of incapacity, but it cannot afford to retain incapacity.

But, beyond all this, there is much to be accomplished by the Constituencies themselves. The individuals of the several parties invariably sent for on any change of Ministry to form a Government are apparently limited in the choice of colleagues to a very narrow circle. The distribution of offices may be altered, but – with now and then an exception, and often a very ill-chosen and ill-placed exception – the same set of men, or at all events the same names and connexions, be they Liberals or Conservatives, hold, parliament after parliament, the entire governing power. The idea prevails that there are no men in the kingdom to take their places; that they, and they only, can command sufficient influence to give Government a majority in the Lords and Commons whilst Parliament sits, and a majority in the country at a general election. The candidates sent down from the Clubs are chosen with the constant object of upholding, whether in or out of office, the fixed Ministerial cliques. Upon Members so selected, the party circle has a continual hold; it is thus of the utmost importance, that the Electors in every borough and county should put an end to the system under which, not the constituencies, but the Clubs, choose who shall be members, and what places they shall represent. The Association would, therefore, urge the Electors, in all earnestness, to select their own candidates. It is an essential step in Administrative Reform, that the Constituencies shall shake off the Clubs and their Agents. There is nothing in an election to require the assistance of a Parliamentary trafficker in seats.

Electors, if you would have an honest Government, you must choose your members honestly, and must set your faces determinedly against that disgraceful system which spends fortunes upon elections; you must resolve also, in earnest, to put an end to election corruption. *It is this that keeps aloof from Parliament your ablest men; they do not choose to be defeated, – they will not condescend to the conditions of success.* Means must be found to correct this grievous evil – the nation cannot afford to have its representation jobbed, and its best men deterred from Parliament.

With these objects before them, the Association invite every Constituency in the kingdom to make themselves acquainted with the opinions of their Representatives upon Administrative Reform; to call upon them to support in Parliament every question bearing upon the subject; to hold meetings; to organise local committees; to enrol members; to collect funds; to put themselves in immediate communication with the Committee in London; to be ready for an election – ready with worthy candidates, an honest Committee, and a thorough determination to have done with the abuses of elections.

Fellow-Countrymen, we have reached a turning point in our national history; we know now that we can go on no longer as we have done – that, following the beaten track, we are no longer sure of our position. We must either work out a thorough change, or take a lower grade in the world. But there is no ground for despondency: the nation is not worn out – the people were never more strong of purpose, more sound at heart, more united in opinion: it is the rulers and the system, "*the torpid hands of Government,*" that have failed us, not the people. Let the nation, therefore, "bend its whole force to the reduction of that corrupt influence which is itself the perennial spring of all prodigality and of all disorder, which loads us with debt, which takes away vigour from our arms, wisdom from our councils, and every shadow of authority and credit from the most venerable parts of our constitution." Let the nation resolve that there shall be a searching and complete Administrative Reform, "that the right men shall be in the right places," and there is nothing to apprehend for the position of England.

13

EXTRACT FROM *SECULARISM IN ITS VARIOUS RELATIONS*

Charles Watts

Source: *Secularism in Its Various Relations*, 1875, pp. 45–46

We have to disestablish and disendow the State Church, applying the vast national endowments to national education, instead of non-national mis-education. Those who are enamoured of Bishops, Deans, Archdeacons, Prebendaries, Canons, and such-like sumptuous officers of the Church Militant, whose fighting is chiefly within itself, may support the same in such luxury as they please, and as long as they like, out of their own pockets, not at the expense of us all; just as Dissenters support their own ministers, and Secularists their own lecturers, when they care enough for their principles, and the men suit their taste. With the disestablishment of the Church, its lordly Bishops must evacuate the Upper House, where they are quite misplaced, and only do mischief to themselves and the nation. We have to educate and enfranchise the masses of the people, kept ignorant and disenfranchised all these centuries back by the physical and mental tyranny of Feudalism and Ecclesiasticism, of Statecraft and Priestcraft, whose hopeful motto comes from the Bible: "Fear God and honour the King." We find no God to fear, and we want no King to honour above ourselves. The Education on which we insist must be free, compulsory, universal, and Secular. Those who want their children taught some religion can arrange for this at home, or elsewhere, out of school hours; the teaching for which the nation provides must be of subjects which all the nation recognises as useful, and these subjects are strictly secular. We have also to rescue the Endowed Schools, which remain monopolised by the Church, to keep from its clutches those which are partially rescued, and to make these institutions do useful work in something like a fair proportion to the funds and appliances at their command. We have to remove all legal disabilities founded on sex, adult suffrage with us meaning man and woman suffrage. Although the Christians are fond of boasting that their religion has elevated woman, we know that the New Testament, as well as the Old, distinctly proclaims her inferiority and subservience to man. With our belief that all human beings have an equal right to the full development and the free exercise of their faculties, we are bound to open to women as to men all spheres of activity. They will succeed in those for which they are fit, they will fail in those for which they are not fit; it is waste of time to discuss beforehand their fitness or unfitness for this or that; it is absurd as it is unjust to hinder them from trying at what they will. We have to reform our electoral system; redistribute seats, approximate to equality of representation, extend and improve the representation of minorities, facilitate the election of eminent or eminently representative men. At present five million Roman Catholics in England may not secure a single seat for a representative of their religion, because, being scattered throughout the country, they have not a majority in any one borough or country; while a local magnate, to whom all the rest of the country is contemptuously and justly indifferent, may be returned by the votes of two or three hundred neighbours, who are virtually his dependents. We have to abolish the House of Lords as an hereditary legislature. If a Second Chamber is advisable, in order to obviate head-long legislation in times of excitement, let it be a real Senate of the approved notables of the country, the most eminent and experienced men of whatever class or profession, who are able and willing thus to serve the public. We have to make such changes in the Land Laws that, while the landholder shall be treated with fair consideration, the nation shall have its just interest in its own mother-earth, and its befitting control over the transmission of property in the same, and over its general cultivation. We have to do away with, as gently as possible, the preposterously costly and useless Monarchy. It may be becoming for a ship to have a gilded figure-head; but who ever heard of a nautical figure-head whose gilding cost the seventieth part of the whole working expenses of the ship, and which, moreover, had the property of producing little figure-heads, each of which, as it grew up, wanted its own lavish gilding? And who ever heard of a figure-head being gilded annually at this prodigal rate, while in fact it was never exposed at the bow of the ship, but secluded under a glass case, and muffled in heavy draperies from the eyes of the vulgar, from year's beginning to year's end?

14

THE MILITANT METHODS OF THE NWSPU

Christabel Pankhurst

Source: Speech at St. James's Hall, 15 October 1908

THE BYE-ELECTION POLICY

What means do we use? What kind of unconstitutional methods do we employ? Well, it sounds rather Irish to say that one of our unconstitutional means is a very constitutional one. It consists in asking men for the kind loan of their vote; that is to say, that at every bye-election we urge the electors to help us by voting against the Government. Is our opposition to the Government effective? Do we turn votes? Well, ask that question of any Liberal candidate. Why, in the first place, the poor man cannot even get an audience! The electors would rather listen to us, because, you see, our question is a living one. The people want to hear about votes for women. They are rather tired of the dry-as-dust political speeches that the ordinary politicians offer to them. They are much more interested in this "side issue," as politicians are fond of calling the votes for women question. A side issue in a politician's mouth means, you know, a question that he prefers the electors not to take any notice of, and when, as is the case nowadays, it is said on the defeat of a Liberal candidate, that side issues had much to do with that defeat, you may know that "votes for women" has been the real issue of the election! You must have noticed, too, frequent denunciations by Liberal candidates and their supporters of the "outside organisations" which enter the field at each bye-election in opposition to the Government, and one Member of the Government, Lord Crewe, has said that their activity must be suppressed by law. I can assure them that they will find it impossible to prevent the Women's Social and Political Union, which is the most important and active of these "outside organisations," from putting a finger in the pie at election times. We will allow no Act of Parliament to restrain us from making our appeal to a higher power than the Government themselves. We cannot get justice from the Government – the inferior court; we will appeal, even if it means imprisonment, against their decision, to a higher court, to the electors. Yes, if the present Government – who, after all, are the servants of the people – if they deny us justice, we shall, whatever repressive measures may be used against us, call for the support of the men who have votes. But we are interested and encouraged by the proposal in question. We know perfectly well that the outside organisation which they fear the most, that they fear more than all the others put together, is the Women's Social and Political Union. As yet they do not openly admit it. Ask a Liberal Member of Parliament whether we prevent the election of Liberal candidates. He will say, "Oh, no; nonsense. These women have no influence at all on the elections." Well, I ask you, why not? These Members of Parliament think they have influence themselves. They speak in support of their friend, the Liberal candidate, at a bye-election, and they think they can turn votes. Well, I am sure that the women in our Union can turn votes if they can! We are as good speakers as the men. We know as much about politics. We are not so vain as to suppose that it is by our own ability; we know it is by the greatness of our cause that we win our way in this country. It is the strength rather than the manner of our appeal that turns votes against the Government. Now, we have got a good cause, while the Liberal Party have a bad cause. So, of course, we defeat the Government at bye-elections. I have not time to lay before you all the evidence on this point, but I will give you the evidence of a Liberal Member of Parliament. Sir Charles Maclaren has publicly stated that we women are responsible for the Government defeats which have been attributed to the work of the Tariff Reformers. Well, now, let us convince our Liberal friends that it is no good trying to hide their heads in the sand. If we are influencing the electorate, we are influencing it, and no amount of denying that fact will make any difference. Liberals are apt to refuse to see a thing until it hits them in the eye. They did not believe there was a Labour Party until thirty Labour Members walked into the House of Commons. And they are now trying to believe that there is no women's movement. But this, like other illusions, will disappear as they find it more and more impossible to get elected to the House of Commons, because the women are there, barring the door against them.

Well now, that is what the men do to help us: they vote against the Government because the Government deny us political justice. How have we gained the support of men? It is by the militant methods that we have done it. It used to be said that we were alienating the country; but it is now recognised that by the new methods we have roused a feeling of chivalry in the electors and have stirred them to help us. It is quite true that when we began the militant campaign people did not understand, but now the people are with us – with us in our demand and with us in what we do to press it forward. And as we rise in the public esteem, the Government and their supporters fall. Knowing that we have the people with us, we are prepared to look our enemy straight in the face, and to fight him with more skill and more vigour and more enthusiasm than ever. The sight of women fighting for their rights, disregarding risks, hardships, penalties, has fired the imagination, touched the hearts of the people, and finally won them over to our cause. Their love of fair play, their admiration of a good fighting spirit, their desire to see the right triumph, are making them stand for us and against the Government. We have not alienated the people, we have won them by the militant methods.

PROTESTS AT CABINET MINISTERS' MEETINGS

Apart from the opposition to the Government at bye-elections, we have two other means of attack. First, there are protests at Cabinet Ministers' meetings, and most useful and effective those protests are. This same method was adopted by men before they got the vote. In addition, they went in for storming the platform, and sending Cabinet Ministers flying in danger of their lives. We have a little more mercy for the enemy, but we adopt the same tactics in a modified form. We make no apology for doing this; we know it to be both necessary and right. Cabinet Ministers complain of being thus treated, but let them give women the vote. To deny us justice and whine at the consequent punishment is undignified and poor-spirited. Dr. Cooper, a Liberal Member of the present Parliament, tells us that, "Before the Reform Bill was carried, not a single opponent of Men's Suffrage could get in a word at a public meeting." We ourselves are not afraid of interruptions. We go out into the market-place and we speak to our countrymen and women. We are not afraid of them; we are not afraid of their opposition. We meet it fairly. We win them over by argument. Why do not Cabinet Ministers try that method? If they were prepared with an answer to our question, "Will you give women the vote?" all would be well. But because they will not give that answer they fear our question. They are not prepared to do us justice, and, you know, the knowledge that he is in the wrong makes anybody a coward. They can win us over by giving us the vote. And, my friends, the straits to which they are reduced are really extraordinary. They dare not face a public meeting, so their meetings are packed. In fact, in the matter of packed meetings the Liberal Party have broken the record. They can never more abuse the Tory Party; Tories have never gone to such lengths in order to escape their political opponents. Not long ago we protested at a Peace meeting addressed by a member of the Government. From this, as from other Cabinet Ministers' meetings, our members were violently ejected. The question of peace is of vital interest to women; and the question of national defence is of vital interest to us. Do we escape scot-free if the country is invaded? The questions discussed at that meeting were women's questions; and before very long we women must have the vote and take our part in deciding these great issues. When we see possible war and bloodshed ahead, do not you think that, as public-spirited human beings, we ought to fight for the vote as we have never fought for it before? Well, we went to the Peace meeting – and we did not find that the principles of peace were carried into practice. Never mind, we do not complain of that. Unlike the Prime Minister, we do not want artificial protection. We are ready to face the hardships of political life, while these frail men, the members of the Liberal Government, cannot bear to hear a word of opposition to them.

Members of the Union lately attended a Liberal meeting at Swansea. Some of us have been accused of inciting to violence. Well, we will not say more of that just now, but I want you to notice this – that Liberal Cabinet Ministers have set us a very bad example. At our meetings, when a man interrupts – as he very often does – you do not hear us say to the stewards: "He must be ruthlessly flung out."

No; we leave that to Mr. Lloyd George. But I want to point out to you that when a man in his position uses such words, it is taken by the ordinary unthinking hooligan to mean that he can do what he likes to the suffragettes. If the Government had not used force against us, if they had not had us arrested and imprisoned, if they had not insulted us by charging us with being hirelings, by telling stewards to throw us out, we should not have been in the daily physical danger that some of our women are in. We have been brought up to believe – some of us – that men's desire was to protect women from the hurly-burly and dangers of life; and yet, although Members of the present Government know that by denying us the vote and applying methods of coercion to us, they are placing us in danger of life and limb every day that we live, they continue to refuse our demand. In their own defence, however, they do not hesitate to collect 6,000 policemen, leaving the rest of London at the mercy of robbers and thieves.

My friends, before I leave this question of protesting at meetings, I will tell you why we do it. We do it, in the first place, to draw attention to our grievance and to educate the public. Cabinet Ministers will not do this for us – they shirk this question – we have got to do it for ourselves. In the second place, we know it to be an excellent way of harassing Cabinet Ministers. It is nothing to us to be interrupted, but to them it is a very serious matter. You see, they have not the sense of humour that we have got, and that means that they have no sense of proportion. Therefore Cabinet Ministers think their own speeches of vast importance. They like to deliver those speeches to a unanimous and enthusiastic audience, and as they cannot secure such an audience at an ordinary public meeting, they try to secure it by packing their meetings with partisans. They are bent on getting this unanimous support, even if it is a little artificial in its character. On the day following their meeting they like to read in the press verbatim accounts of what they said, and it makes them feel a bit sore when they find there is more in the newspapers about what the women have said than about what they have said themselves. When they get to the House of Commons – well, you know what men are about ridicule; they cannot bear it. They are very much like a pack of schoolboys in the House of Commons, you know; they tease each other so. Then they cannot go to the club or anywhere without receiving humorous condolences on account of the trouble they have had with the suffragettes. I need not say more. Everybody who knows what kind of persons these politicians are will realise what a very good idea it is to go and make protests at their meetings.

DEPUTATIONS TO THE HOUSE OF COMMONS

Next we must consider the deputations to the House of Commons. Recently we approached the House supported by thousands of the citizens of London. If men took this means of influencing Parliament it would be wrong, and I will tell you why – because they have representatives sitting in the House of Commons. It is right for us to do it; it is our duty to do it. It would be wrong for us not to do it, because we have nobody to represent us inside the House. If the House of

Commons had any sense of logic, they would understand this point. The whole world, apart from them, understands it; and I do not – I will tell you between ourselves – I do not despair of succeeding, by constant repetition of an obvious fact, of driving that fact inside the minds of Members of Parliament. There have been leading articles in the newspapers condemning our recent action. Nobody else except the writers of those articles (perhaps not even they) has this opinion. As a matter of fact, those leading articles are most encouraging – among the best things that we have had yet. Why, they are the next best thing to getting the vote! When we are told that we are a nuisance, that we are upsetting London, that we ought to be put down with a strong hand – well, we are not far from victory.

15

THE STRUGGLE FOR POLITICAL LIBERTY

Chrystal Macmillan

Source: Speech, 16 February 1909

When the history of the twentieth century comes to be written it will be told how its first years witnessed a great revival of interest in and enthusiasm for the fundamental principles of liberty, and freedom and justice, an awakening to the fact that, if in theory men hold these things good for all, in practice they are a monopoly of certain privileged classes. This awakening is not confined to one country nor to one race. The Russians, the Turks, the Persians, the Indians have realised that it is not consistent with their dignity as rational and moral beings that they should be compelled to obey laws they have no share in making, or that they should be denied the responsibility of shaping the destinies of their countries. The unrepresented in these countries have risen and demanded recognition, and in a certain measure the authorities have yielded to their just claim. To Russia and Turkey have been granted constitutions, with partial freedom of representation, and to the Indians a larger share in the government of their great country.

But when time has brought us to a point where we shall be able to see the events of to-day in a truer perspective, the struggles and victories of the men of these countries will sink into insignificance beside the struggle for freedom which women are now waging in all the so-called civilised countries of the world. The efforts of these men will but take their places as parallel to similar efforts in which the governed have asserted their right as "the people" against the assumed divine right of those holding hereditary power. The plebeians of Rome fought that they might be represented by Tribunes of their own choosing; the Barons at Runnymede compelled an unwilling king to sign away his hereditary power; the people of England did not let the divine right of Charles I. save him from the scaffold; the clamour of the people forced the landlord House of Commons of 1832 to share its hereditary power with a large unrepresented class.

These struggles have many points of similarity. In all, those born to the ruling class unwillingly yield to the pressure of the people. They resist always in the belief that they are acting only for the good of the people, and as anxious to save them from responsibility; while the people insist that they best know what is for their own good, and claim the right to share in the responsibility of governing themselves. The governing class bases its hereditary claim on the natural or the divine order of things, and shuts its eyes to the fact that what it takes for a natural order is merely a passing political custom. The people assert that the natural qualification for taking a share in the government is simply that they are the people for whom the Government exists.

Women in their fight have all these difficulties to face; for men, who are the ruling power to-day, are unwilling to share that power with the women of the country. Men resist the claims of the women professedly on the ground that they are acting, not only for the good of the country in general, but for the good of the women themselves, and because they are anxious to save the women from responsibility. The men base their claim on the natural order of things – sometimes even on the divine order – forgetting that their right is merely hereditary and founded on custom, and that what seems to their limited outlook the natural order of things is no more than a political custom of their own time and country.

But over and above, women have to face the further difficulty that they are as yet unrecognised as "the people." Women in all countries are realising this. They are rising, and not only are they organising in their separate countries but they are organising internationally. At the conference in Amsterdam in 1908 twenty-one different countries were represented. Delegates were present from all parts of the world – from the United States and Canada, from South Africa and Australia, from Spain and Russia, from Bohemia and Bulgaria – and from women of all nationalities it was possible to realise how widespread is the agitation and how the suffrage is everywhere considered the fundamental question. Though so many different races and countries were represented, the remarkable fact is that, just as in this country, the Women's Suffrage Societies, whether constitutional or militant, party or non-party, unite in the form of their demand; so all these different countries make the same demand – in the words of their resolution, "to ask for the franchise on the same terms as it is now, or may be, exercised by men," leaving any required extension to be decided by the men and women together. Be the franchise wide or be it limited, it must not exclude women on the ground of sex. In other words, women demand that they should be recognised as "the people."

Part 3
REPRESENTATION

16

'ADMISSION OF BARON DE ROTHSCHILD'

Source: House of Commons, 26 July 1858

MR. SPEAKER Any hon. Member who desires to take his seat will please come to the table to be sworn.

BARON LIONEL NATHAN DE ROTHSCHILD returned as one of the Members for the City of London, came to the table, and was about to take from the Clerk at the table a copy of the Oath prescribed by the 21 & 22 Vict., c. 48, passed this Session, when

MR. WARREN rose and said: Mr. Speaker, I rise to order. I wish to ask you, Sir, whether notice was not necessary before – ["Order! Chair!"] Sir, I rise to order –

MR. SPEAKER Order, order! The taking of his seat by an hon. Member is matter of privilege, and ought not to be interrupted by any discussion whatever.

The prescribed form of oath was again tendered to BARON DE ROTHSCHILD by the Clerk,

BARON LIONEL DE ROTHSCHILD Sir, I beg to state that, being a person professing the Jewish religion, I entertain a conscientious objection to take the oath which, by an Act passed in the present Session, has been substituted for the oaths of Allegiance, Supremacy, and Abjuration, in the form therein required.

Whereupon the Clerk reported the matter to Mr. SPEAKER, who desired Baron LIONEL NATHAN DE ROTHSCHILD to withdraw; and he withdrew accordingly.

LORD JOHN RUSSELL My object in rising, Sir, is to move a Resolution in conformity with an Act recently passed. (21 & 22 Vict. c. 49). It is as follows: – That it appears to this House that Baron Lionel Nathan de Rothschild, a person professing the Jewish Religion, being otherwise entitled to sit and vote in this House, is prevented from so sitting and voting by his conscientious objection to take the Oath which, by an Act passed in the present Session of Parliament, has been substituted for the Oaths of Allegiance, Supremacy, and Abjuration, in the form therein required.

MR. J. A. SMITH seconded the Resolution.

Question proposed.

MR. WARREN Mr. Speaker, it is with great reluctance and regret, and contrary to my own previously-declared determination not to open my lips again on this question, that I rise to address a few observations to the House. It has now arrived at a very grave crisis in its constitutional history and that of the country, and a sense of duty will not allow me to remain silent. I have already, and very lately, as an humble member of the great Conservative party, entered my most solemn protest against the step which the Legislature was about to take in this matter, and have but little to say upon this momentous occasion. This House is about to consummate that great constitutional change in the character of the House which it has so lately been empowered to effect, and to take upon itself the entire responsibility of admitting into the representative branch of the Legislature a gentleman who has this moment declared that he cannot take – that he cannot be bound by an oath administered on the Holy Gospels – an oath which has been so long taken by all other Members of this House, with the exception of those who, though Christians by profession, were permitted, in deference to their religious scruples, to use a different form of oath or declaration. Sir, this is to me a most painful and distressing moment – but I cannot help myself; and, in accordance with what my conscience tells me is my most imperative duty, I am resolved to take the sense of the House upon the proposed Resolution. Lest, however, any one should do me the grievous injustice of supposing that I am, at a moment so painful, actuated by considerations of a personal nature with respect to either Baron Rothschild or the ancient race to which he belongs, I beg now most emphatically and truly to disclaim any such feelings. With reference to that gentleman, I must take this opportunity of declaring, that never in my life did I hear a whisper of even an insinuation against his character – of anything inconsistent with that reputation for purity, that spotlessness of character which Baron Rothschild enjoys. He occupies, deservedly, a high social position in this country; and I can only say again, that, while compelled to oppose the Resolution of the noble Lord opposite – to resist him to the last on this question – I have not in my heart one particle of animosity towards either the Jewish race or that representative of it now seeking admission into this Christian Legislature. If it be really the deliberate will of this House of Commons, as it has undoubtedly been declared the will of the Imperial Legislature that they may, if they think fit, exercise a privilege which I for one regard as so dangerous, I have nothing more to say; but in the meantime I beg, though I should go out alone into the lobby, to meet the Resolution of the noble Lord with a direct negative.

MR. WALPOLE I do not think my hon. and learned Friend could have caught correctly the terms of the noble Lord's Resolution. It is simply declaratory, in terms of the new Act, of a matter of fact which neither my hon. and learned Friend nor any one else will contest, and does not admit either Baron Rothschild or any other member of the Jewish persuasion to a seat in this House. I hope, therefore, that my hon. and learned Friend will not put the House to the trouble of dividing at the present stage of the proceedings.

MR. WARREN I am much obliged to my right hon. Friend, and shall not press for a division on this Resolution. I had not caught the exact words of it and was taken altogether by surprise by the whole proceedings of this morning. I therefore withdraw my Motion.

Resolved, – That it appears to this House that Baron Lionel de Rothschild, a person professing the Jewish Religion, being otherwise entitled to sit and vote in this House, is prevented from so sitting and voting by his conscientious objection to take the Oath which, by an Act passed in the present Session of Parliament, has been substituted for the Oaths of Allegiance, Supremacy, and Abjuration, in the form therein required.

LORD JOHN RUSSELL I now rise, Sir, to move a Resolution in pursuance of the Act which received the assent of Her Majesty on the 23rd instant, and which is entitled "An Act to provide for the relief of Her Majesty's subjects professing the Jewish religion." In order that the House may be fully in possession of the words of the Act I shall now read them. By the first clause it is enacted that – Where it shall appear to either House of Parliament that a person professing the Jewish religion, otherwise entitled to sit and vote in such House, is prevented from so sitting and voting by his conscientious objection to take the Oath which by an Act passed or to be passed in the present Session of Parliament has been or may be substituted for the Oaths of Allegiance, Supremacy, and Abjuration, in the form therein required, such House, if it think fit, may resolve that thenceforth any person professing the Jewish religion, in taking the said Oath to entitle him to sit and vote as aforesaid, may omit the words 'and I make this declaration upon the true faith of a Christian.' It is not necessary to read any further. I propose, in conformity with those words in the clause, "such House, if it think fit," to move a Resolution as nearly as possible in the terms of the Act itself. Of course, I shall not now raise any question as to whether a Jew should sit in this House. That question has been repeatedly argued, and it has now been decided by Parliament, at least to the extent of leaving it to either House to act as it may think fit. I therefore content myself with moving: "That any person professing the Jewish Religion may henceforth, in taking the Oath prescribed in an Act of the present Session of Parliament to entitle him to sit and vote in this House, omit the words 'and I make this declaration upon the true faith of a Christian.'"

MR. J. A. SMITH seconded the Resolution.

Motion made and Question put, That any person professing the Jewish Religion may henceforth, in taking the Oath prescribed in an Act of the present Session of Parliament to entitle him to sit and vote in this House, omit the words, 'and I make this declaration upon the true faith of a Christian.'

MR. WARREN Now, Sir, the time has arrived at which I may make my Motion, and state that I shall take the sense of the House upon it. It is, of course, not necessary for me to repeat any of the observations I have already offered, but must beg the House to regard them as having been offered in opposition to the noble Lord's present Resolution, which I now meet with a direct negative.

LORD HOTHAM Sir, I do not intend to occupy the time of the House for more than one or two moments. My object is simply to explain the reasons of the Vote which I shall feel it my duty to give. I have always found myself conscientiously under the necessity of opposing the admission to Parliament of persons professing the Jewish religion. I have done so upon principle, and without the slightest particle of personal feeling. As Parliament, however, has decided against my views of this matter, I did not come down to the House to record any further vote on this question, but to take part in the discussion of other business; but, being here, I have to consider what course I ought to pursue. The part I have hitherto taken renders it impossible for me to concur in the Resolution of the noble Lord; while I cannot withdraw and abstain from giving any vote upon the question. I do not think it would be either an honest or a straightforward mode of proceeding, to shrink from expressing my opinion on a subject, with reference to which I think so strongly. I am therefore reduced to the necessity, without the slightest personal feeling towards Baron Rothschild, of going into the lobby with those who are resolved to meet the Resolution with a direct negative.

MR. HADFIELD said, he had never been able to account for the prejudice which influenced hon. Gentlemen opposite in their hostility to the Jews. In his opinion the world was more indebted to that particular family of the human race than any other nation or people that ever existed. Hon. Gentlemen talked of excluding the Jews as a matter of Christian principle. He would say, let them endeavour to Christianize themselves by following the example of Him they all reverenced as the great messenger of peace, charity, and toleration, and who directed that the Gospel should be preached to all men – but to the Jew first. He regretted that this prejudice towards that family of the human race, to whom we were so deeply indebted, should have so long continued, but rejoiced in the opportunity of taking part in the removal of the Just of the disabilities which that prejudice had in this country inflicted upon them. He looked upon that occasion as a great triumph for the cause of religious liberty.

MR. WALPOLE Sir, when first this question was brought before the House expressed my opinion, and I have never shrunk from that opinion since, that it was a religious rather than a political question. I thought from the first that the Legislature of this country, being admittedly a Christian Legislature from the earliest time, was not a body into which a person professing the Jewish religion could properly or conscientiously be admitted. I merely mention that for the purpose of showing, that now that the time has come for this House to determine how it will act, it is impossible for me not to feel, while admitting that Parliament has given us the power to seat Baron Rothschild on our own responsibility, that considering the opinions I have always held, I cannot be a party to the proposed Resolution. One or two words more and I have done, for I do not wish to raise any controversy on this occasion. I cannot disguise from myself that the person whom the House is now about to seat has this very much in his favour – that throughout the whole of this controversy he has never attempted to act in a manner contrary to the law of the land or to the rules of this House. I think it due to Baron Rothschild that I should say so much. I agree in the observations made by my noble Friend (Lord Hotham) when stating the reasons which would compel him to vote against this Resolution, and I shall go into the lobby with my noble Friend. There is one other observation that I would make. The hon. Members who advocate the admission of the Jews think that they are now closing this matter; but in point of fact they are not. The course taken by Parliament in reference to this question is a course which in my opinion cannot be too much deprecated. I, for one, am extremely sorry that if Baron Rothschild, and those who like him, profess the Jewish religion, were to be admitted into the Legislature at all, they were not admitted frankly, plainly, and honestly, by a declaration made by Parliament in the form of an Act of the Legislature, instead of in a mode which I am afraid we shall hereafter find cause to regret.

MR. SPOONER Sir, the hon. Member for Sheffield has charged those who oppose the admission of the Jews into Parliament as so acting in consequence of a prejudice against the Jewish people. I, for one, utterly deny that. The Jews are a most interesting nation – interesting, if we look to their past history, and more so if we contemplate their future destiny. No, Sir, we are not actuated by any prejudice against the Jewish people as a nation, or from personal objection to the respectable individual who now presents himself for admission. There cannot be a second opinion with regard to that gentleman personally. He has the respect and esteem of all who know him, and especially of those who possess his friendship. What does actuate those who oppose such admission is the full and decided conviction that a Christian assembly like this Legislature should be wholly Christian, if we expect what we pray for – the blessing of Almighty God on our exertions to properly direct the affairs of a free and Christian people. The hon. Member for Sheffield (Mr. Hadfield) who so much rejoices at the House of Lords having given their consent to the admission of Jews to this House by a simple Resolution, has not made one word of objection to the Reasons which came down from that House for having rejected that clause of the Bill which permitted the Jew to take his seat in this House – which Reasons declared, in emphatic terms, that the Jew was morally unfit to sit and legislate in a Christian Legislature. I beg to express my full concurrence in those Reasons, and therefore I cannot give my vote for admitting a person whom those Reasons declare to be totally unfit for admission into this House.

...

Question put, That any person professing the Jewish Religion may henceforth, in taking the Oath prescribed in an Act of the present Session of Parliament to entitle him to sit and vote in this House, omit the words, 'and I make this declaration upon the true faith of a Christian.'

The House divided: – Ayes 69; Noes 37; Majority 32 . . .

BARON LIONEL NATHAN DE ROTHSCHILD being again come to the Table, desired to be sworn on the Old Testament, as being binding on his conscience: – Whereupon the Clerk reported the matter to Mr. Speaker, who then desired the Clerk to swear him upon the Old Testament.

BARON LIONEL NATHAN DE ROTHSCHILD was sworn accordingly, and subscribed the Oath at the Table.

17

'INDIAN TAXATION'

Sir Mancherjee Bhownaggree

Source: House of Commons, 3 September 1895

MR. M. M. BHOWNAGGREE (Bethnal Green, N.E.) in a maiden speech, seconded the Motion. He said he did so unhesitatingly, because the burden on the Indian taxpayer had grown in recent years to an enormous extent. But he should disclaim any connection between the Motion and recent events in Chitral. The word "annexation" had been used in connection with Chitral in the course of the Debate; and it was well to point out that it was not very applicable. It was only recently that Sir George Robertson put upon the throne of Chitral its own proper Mehtar, which showed that Chitral was not completely annexed, in the same sense as Burmah was annexed. But, at the same time, it could not be denied that recent events in Chitral, the glorious achievements of our Army, British and Indian, and the prudent resolution of the Government to retain its hold on Chitral, were capable of being read by ambitious military officers in a somewhat different light from that in which they were regarded on the floor of the House of Commons. Many of the difficulties of the Government of India could be traced to this cause. Ambitious officers had before now embroiled themselves in matters which had made it impossible for the Government to escape being brought into conflict with tribes on the frontier. In order, therefore, that the resolution of the Government to retain Chitral, and the approval of the feats of our Army in that region, might not mislead such officers to follow the same course in the future, and also for the reason that there might not be aroused in India an apprehension that the policy of the present Government was annexation, and that they were determined to advance the frontier of India to the furthest limits, and thereby make the burden of the taxpayer so intolerable that India would be plunged into bankruptcy, he begged to second the Motion.

18

'LIQUOR TRAFFIC (RESTRICTIONS)'

Viscountess (Nancy) Astor

Source: House of Commons, 24 February 1920

I shall not begin by craving the indulgence of the House. I am only too conscious of the indulgence and the courtesy of the House. I know that it was very difficult for some hon. Members to receive the first lady M.P. into the House. [HON. MEMBERS: "Not at all!"] It was almost as difficult for some of them as it was for the lady M.P. herself to come in. Hon. Members, however, should not be frightened of what Plymouth sends out into the world. After all, I suppose when Drake and Raleigh wanted to set out on their venturesome careers, some cautious person said, "Do not do it; it has never been tried before. You stay at home, my sons, cruising around in home waters." I have no doubt that the same thing occurred when the Pilgrim Fathers set out. I have no doubt that there were cautious Christian brethren who did not understand their going into the wide seas to worship God in their own way. But, on the whole, the world is all the better for those venturesome and courageous west country people, and I would like to say that I am quite certain that the women of the whole world will not forget that it was the fighting men of Devon who dared to send the first woman to represent women in the Mother of Parliaments. Now, as the west country people are a courageous lot, it is only right that one of their representatives should show some courage, and I am perfectly aware that it does take a bit of courage to address the House on that vexed question, Drink. However, I dare do it. The hon. Member (Sir J. D. Rees) is more than polite. In fact, I should say that he goes almost a bit too far. However. I will consider his proposal if I can convert him.

The issue raised by the hon. Member is really quite clear, although I admit that he did not make it as clear as I would have liked. Do we want the welfare of the community, or do we want the prosperity of the Trade? Do we want national efficiency, or do we want national inefficiency? That is what it comes to. So I hope to be able to persuade the House. Are we really trying for a better world, or are we going to slip back to the same old world before 1914? I think that the hon. Member is not moving with the times. He speaks of vexatious laws and restrictions. I quite agree with him that most laws are vexatious. When we want to go 50 or 60 miles an hour down the Bath Road it is very tiresome, when we come to a village, to have to go 10 miles an hour. Why do we have to do it? It is for the good of the community. We might kill children. He talks about the restrictions. I maintain that they brought a great deal of good to the community. There were two gains. First, there were the moral gains. I should like to tell you about them. The convictions of drunkenness among women during the War were reduced to one-fifth after these vexatious restrictions were brought in. I take women, because, as the hon. Member has said, most of the men were away fighting. Does the House realise what that means? The convictions of drunkenness among women were reduced to one-fifth at a time when many women, thousands of them, were earning more than they had ever dreamed of earning in their lives, which generally means, so they say in industrial communities, that there is more spent on drink. Also women were going through not only a physical strain but the most awful mental tortures. Then the deaths from delirium tremens were greatly reduced. I do not know whether hon. Members have seen the tortures of delirium tremens, but it is a national gain if you can reduce them. The deaths of children from over-laying were halved. That was after these vexatious restrictions were brought in.

These are some of the gains that you can set out on paper. I could talk for five hours on the moral gains. I will not do it, but I could talk for hours on the moral gains which you cannot put on paper, they are so enormous. I am perfectly certain, if hon. Members would really stop to think, that they would not cavil at these vexatious restrictions. Already, we have lost some of these gains. The convictions among women have doubled in the last year since the restrictions have been slightly modified, and they are four times as many among men. That is something that I should like the House to think of. Think what these increased convictions mean. Just think, twice as many convictions among women! Does the House realise what that means? How I wish that I was really an orator. I would like to tell you about drink. I have as good a sense of humour as any other hon. Member, but when I think of the ruin and the desolation and the misery which drink brings into the houses of the working men and women as well as of the well-to-do, I find it a little difficult to be humorous. It was only the other day – I had been down to my constituency – that I was coming back from what they call the poorer parts of the town, and I stopped outside a public house where I saw a child about five years old waiting for its mother. It did not have to wait long. Presently she reeled out. The child went forward to her, but it soon retreated. Oh the oaths and curses of that poor woman and the shrieks of that child as it fled from her. That is not an easy thing to forget. That is what goes on when you have increased drunkenness among women. I am thinking of the women and children. I am not so tremendously excited about what you call the freedom of the men. The men will get their freedom. I do not want to rob them of anything that is good. I only want to ask them to consider others. There is a story – no, I had better not give it. I do not really want to harrow the feelings of the House! But I do want hon. Members to think about these things. What really happens? It is a most terrible thing to talk about it. The freedom of the subject! We, the women, know, and the men know, thousands of us in the country who work amongst the slums, and in prisons and hospitals, we know where John Barleycorn, as you are pleased to call him, leads to. It is not to Paradise. It promises Heaven, and too often it leads to Hell. I will not go on, because it would not be quite fair; but I do beg hon. Members to think of these things, and when they are talking about freedom, to think of the children.

After all, the thought of every man for himself is a thoroughly materialistic doctrine. There is a doctrine of going out to look for the lost sheep; I feel somehow that that is a better spirit to go on with than to be always clamouring about the freedom of the subject. We talk about our war gains and efficiency. You talk about liquor control. What was it set up for? It was set up for national efficiency. It was not set up for temperance. It did pretty well. The War Office and the Admiralty both commended the Liquor Control Board for having greatly gained that for which it was set up. No one would call the War Office or the Admiralty Pussyfoots. [HON. MEMBERS: "Hear, hear!"] There are several among them, but you can hardly look upon them as prejudiced Pussyfoots. In 1916 the Liquor Control Board unanimously reported that they had enormously increased efficiency by the Regulations which the hon. Gentleman opposite wants swept away. The Liquor Board said more, and I would like hon. Members who are always talking about national efficiency and economy to think of this. I want to see whether you are in earnest about this matter or whether it is camouflage. The Liquor Control Board said that the State could not get the maximum of efficiency so long as the drink trade was in private hands. That is what they said. Why did they say so? It is simple. You cannot reconcile the interests of the State with the interests of the trade. If you could there never would have been any licensing laws; there would never have been any drink question. Why cannot you reconcile the two? I will tell you. Because, Mr. Deputy-Speaker, the interests of the trade is to sell as much of its goods as possible. No one can say that is to the interest of the State. I do not blame the trade, but one must say that its interest is absolutely opposed to the interest of the State. The real lesson for the country, so far as drink is concerned, is that State Purchase gets the largest amount of progress with the least amount of unrest. That is really what is meant by our War lessons.

The hon. Member spoke of Carlisle. What was the result at Carlisle? The areas all around Carlisle, nearly every one of them, who were originally against the Liquor Control Board's acquisition of the Carlisle area subsequently asked to be taken in. That is really the result of Carlisle. I am glad the hon. Member mentioned Carlisle. I hope someone who follows will deal with all the facts and figures of Carlisle, because they are something of which to be very proud. There are certain things at Carlisle which we are not able to get anywhere else in England. That is wonderful. I could go on for hours but, as I say, having got the indulgence of the House I will not try it too far . . .

I do ask hon. Members not to misread the spirit of the times. Do not go round saying that you want England a country fit for heroes to live in, do not talk about it unless you mean to do it. I do not want to rob the hon. Member opposite of anything that has given him pleasure. I do not really want to take the joy out of the world, or happiness, or anything that really makes for the betterment of the world; but you know, and I know, that drink really promises everything and gives you nothing. You know it, and the House knows it, and the world is beginning to recognise it. We have no right to think of this question in terms of our appetite, and we have to think of it in something bigger than that. I want you to think of the effect of these restrictions in terms of women and babies. Think of the thousands of children whose fathers even had to put up with more than these vexatious restrictions, who laid down their lives. Think of their fatherless children. Supposing they were your children or my children, would you want them to grow up with the trade flourishing? I do not believe the House would. I do not want you to look on your lady Member as a fanatic or a lunatic. I am simply trying to speak for hundreds of women and children throughout the country who cannot speak for themselves. I want to tell you that I do know the working man, and I know that, if you do not try to fool him, if you tell him the truth about drink, he would be as willing as anybody else to put up with so-called vexatious restrictions.

19

'ROYAL PARKS AND PLEASURE GARDENS'

Margaret Wintringham

Source: House of Commons, 11 April 1922

I am moving this reduction in order to call attention to the necessity for employing women police in Hyde Park. The saving mentioned on page 17 of the Estimates under the head of "Hyde Park, Estimated cost of Metropolitan Police" is just over £3,000. This saving is going to be effected probably at the cost of the dismissal of the women police who are at present acting as patrols in Hyde Park. These are trained, picked and efficient women. Their work is to warn girls, take their addresses, and then to threaten them with proceedings – if it comes to that. This is work that must be done in Hyde Park. Men can do it, but the women at present in the police force are better suited to it. They follow up their cases; they visit the women and the girls at home after they have been warned. I do not wish to cast any reflection on the male police; I only ask that their work should continue to be supplemented by that of the women police. The danger to the nation if this work is left undone will be very serious. The Home Secretary himself admits the importance of this supervision, and the benefit it is to the country, and he has suggested that volunteers should do the work. There is no guarantee that volunteers will undertake the work, and every social service backs up the expenditure of this money. Why run the risk which will follow the stopping of the work for the paltry saving of £3,000? If it is necessary to save this money, the reduction should be apportioned between the male and the female officers. Some part of the work of supervision should be left to women; some woman officer should always be in Hyde Park for girls to appeal to in case of need. I ask that a nucleus of women patrols should be left. There is no saving if this reduction is made at the expense of the mischief which may be done if the supervision by these women police is not maintained.

20

'DEBATE ON THE ADDRESS'

Shapurji Saklatvala

Source: House of Commons, 23 November 1922

I shall offer my apologies to you, Sir, as well as to the House, not only for to-night, but I am afraid, for all the nights that I shall be here. I am afraid that I may be misunderstood if I do not acquire what is known as the traditional manner of the House of Commons. We, the 142 who have come here, and I who was but yesterday with the people of Battersea, know the voice and the minds of the people, and we, who have talked outside upon politics and governmental affairs, wish now that the genuine bonâ fide human voice be talked inside, and I would therefore appeal to you, Sir, to realise that if we are found especially wanting in certain mannerisms or if our phraseology is not up to the standard, it is not for want of respect or want of love for any of you, but simply because we of the people shall now require that the people's matters shall be talked in the people's voice.

His Majesty's Gracious Message referred to the question of unemployment. Unemployment prevails largely in the constituency which I represent. The first immediate thing, that is perhaps not of so great consequence from a strictly political point of view, but is of very great consequence from the immediately psychological point of view, is the unfortunate attitude, at the beginning, of the Prime Minister. The Prime Minister says that he believes in the division of labour, and also in assigning responsibility to Ministers. All that may be true. But it is sometimes welcome to the heart of the British people to be heard by the Prime Minister. If they want a deputation is the Prime Minister to be the judge concerning whether a matter is an appropriate matter for the Prime Minister to hear or not, when the people who may be unemployed, who may be hungry, may have a special desire to see the Prime Minister himself? . . .

Coming to the larger problem of unemployment, the Mover and Seconder of the Address pointed out in their speeches what was wanting in the Message. One of our hon. Members referred to the position in Central Europe. Somebody referred to the collapse of the exchanges, and reference was made to the high taxation. All that may be true, but are we to sit in this House and keep on analysing to-day the condition of yesterday, and going on analysing to-morrow the condition of to-day? Are we not determined once for all to analyse the root causes of it all and to apply the remedy which would remove the real evil? It is perhaps an easy thing to-day to talk of the collapse of the exchanges on the Continent of Europe. Have we no right to ask those who have been ruling this country since 1906 until to-day as to what it was which brought about the conditions that produced the collapse of the exchanges of Europe? Have we no right to ask in a similar manner our friends and the Government that is responsible to-day and the Government which was responsible during all these strenuous years of trial throughout the world as to how and why those conditions were produced? It is not satisfactory for us to say to-day that we are suffering because of these conditions. How are the lower exchanges to be set right?

One of our speakers said that the continent of Europe had been impoverished because capital had gone abroad. Who took it abroad? Is it a sign of disservice to the country for enterprising men to take their capital abroad? If that is so, what can be said of private enterprise in Britain itself, and those British citizens who are taking abroad British capital produced by British working men, day after day and year after year? May I point out to the right hon. Gentleman, who to-day deplores the condition into which Europe has been brought by these greedy private enterprisers taking capital abroad, and ask him why over 74 jute mills have been erected in Bengal by British millers and capitalists who had got the capital produced with the hard toil of the workers of Dundee, with the result that to-day we have shut up shop in Dundee and our workers in Bengal are working at from 14s. to 38s. a month and producing for the owners dividends of from 150 per cent, to 400 per cent.? Out of the 124 coal companies in my country, India, I know that 102 have been opened out by British capitalists who have taken capital abroad for these enterprises. If these are the root causes of private enterprise, may we ask our friends not to sit down and not to wait until the great calamity overtakes this country altogether, but to learn lessons from what has happened on the continent, and remove the causes which brought about the conditions which all of us agree are not worthy of any intelligent and civilised human race?

One of my colleagues referred to the position of the trade with India, especially the textile trade, and I understood the Seconder of the Motion to refer to it in passing, showing how it had become impracticable for the Austrians to buy Indian hides and the Germans to buy any Indian cotton, and so forth. I want the House to note, carefully that the loss of trade with India is due to two separate reasons. One has been the desire of the Government in this country, who have always prided themselves as a constitutional nation and Government, to try in the outside world the most unconstitutional method, namely, of dictating Government to peoples in various parts of the world from outside. No Britisher would for a moment tolerate a constitution for Great Britain if it were written outside of Great Britain by people who are not British. In a similar way the constitutions for Ireland and India and Egypt and Mesopotamia should be constitutions written by the men of those countries, in those countries, without interference from outside. But there is another great cause, and I wish the House to understand it clearly. That cause is private enterprise. The story of private enterprise, with all its glamour and its seductive tale, has gone out from these shores to India, and it is the rivalry due to the spirit of private enterprise which is responsible now, and will be responsible in the future, for one country depriving the workers of another country of their legitimate livelihood. It is the growth of this private enterprise, of these large corporations and trusts, these huge industrial concerns in India, which is beginning to tell its tale upon the workers of this country. I wish to make no secret of it. The cotton industry of this country is bound to suffer from this two-fold evil, namely, the political sulking of the people of India with the people of Great Britain, and the spread of private enterprise and of the so-called legitimate privileges of the private enterprisers. The Indian private enterprisers have learned to ask for protective duties, for high dividends, for low wages, long hours, and all kinds of privileges which private enterprise in this country has claimed for 150 years. It is this combination and the spread of the cult of private enterprise by the political bosses in this country which is working the ruin of the workers of this land.

In reference to the Near East there was a passing reference in the Address. I would not like to embarrass either the Government or this House in dealing with the problem of the Near East or the Far East in a thoroughly different manner from that of the past if it be intended so to do. If the Government merely intend to deliver different forms of speeches from those of the past Government they will fail as the last Government failed. I remember the time when a British Prime Minister had to stop a Catholic procession from forming in the streets of Westminster because the Protestants would not allow it. If that happened in the streets of London not many years ago under a Liberal Government, I think that the less the Britisher talks of taking care of the minorities in Armenia or Mesopotamia or Ulster or Southern Ireland or anywhere else, the better it will be for him. There is quite enough for him to take care of in the minorities here. There are many minorities . . .

In reference to Ireland, I am afraid that I shall strike a jarring note in the hitherto harmonious music of this House. I am well disciplined and trained in the general principle of the Labour movement, namely, that the happiness of the world depends on international peace, and that international peace is possible only when the self-determined will of the people of each country prevails in each country. I deplore greatly those elements still existing in the Irish Treaty that are not compatible with that great and wholesome principle. It is no use denying the fact, for we shall not in that way create peace in Ireland. As a House we say that we are giving this Irish Treaty with a view of bringing peace to Ireland, but we know that it is not bringing peace. Either we are actuated by the motive of restoring thorough peace in Ireland or we are doing it as partial conquerors in Ireland. Everyone knows that the Treaty has unfortunately gone forth as the only alternative to a new invasion of Ireland by British troops. As long as that element exists the people of Ireland have a right to say that the very narrow majority which in Ireland accepted the Treaty at the time, accepted it also on this understanding – that if they did not accept it the alternative was an invasion by the Black-and-Tans of this country. The Irish Treaty all along continues to suffer in Ireland from the fact that it is not a Treaty acceptable to the people as a whole.

If it were possible in some way in the preamble of the Treaty or by an Act of this House to allow the people of Ireland to understand that their country's constitution is to be framed by them as a majority may decide, and that the alternative would not be an invasion from this country, but that this, country would shake hands with Ireland as a neighbour, whatever shape or form that Government took, it would be quite a different story. Otherwise, whatever we may do, however many treaties we may pass, however unanimous the British may be in their behaviour towards Ireland, Ireland will not be made a peaceful country. As in 1801 England gave them a forced Union, so in 1922 England is giving them a forced freedom. We must remove that factor. Unless we do so we shall not be giving to the Irish the Treaty of freedom which we have all decided mentally that we are doing. When I say so, I put forward not my personal views but the views of 90 per cent, of those Irishmen who are my electors. They have pointed out to me that, whereas under the threat of renewed invasion the Dail only passed the Treaty by a majority of barely half a dozen votes, Irishmen who are not under that threat – Irishmen who are living in Great Britain – have, by a tremendous majority, voted against it. As long as those factors continue to exist, the Irish Treaty is not going to be what we – in a sort of silent conspiracy – have decided to name it. The reality will not be there. The reality is not there.

Before I conclude I wish to refer to one point which is conspicuous by its absence from the King's Speech. If in the Empire, this House and this Government is going to take the glory of the good, they will also have to take the ignominy of anything disgraceful which happens outside this country. This Government may not be responsible. This House may not be responsible. The people of this country may not be responsible. Yet there is something like a public voice and public prejudice, and if this Government and this House are proud of their association with the Colonies and the Empire, this Government and this House will also have to satisfy this country as well as outside countries, why the policy of the South African Government, in hanging and shooting workers, was permitted and was kept quiet. We are still calling Ireland a part of this Empire, and it is only last week that four young working-class lads, without an open trial and without even fair notice to their families, were shot dead. Even on the night before, their families were told that everything was all right, but on the following morning, when the mother of one of them went to convey a bundle of laundry to her son, she was informed that the poor boys had been executed. These acts might be described as the acts of independent governments. Either these governments are independent or they are part of this Empire. If they are part of this Empire, then the Government in the centre of the Empire must see to it that a policy of this kind does not go without challenge and without, at least, protest from this House, if nothing else can be done.

Our relationship with Russia is also a subject conspicuous by the absence of any mention. We hear of the revolution in Italy; we hear of Mussolini, the leader of it, and we have seen Mussolini's manifesto. He does not care for the Italian Parliament, nor for the majority in it. He is going to rule the country by 300,000 most obedient and faithful followers who are fully armed. Here is a revolutionary. But our Foreign Secretary is sitting in consultation with him. Our Foreign Secretary is shaking hands with him. We do not object on the ground that the Italian Government is a revolutionary Government. Why? Because the revolution in this case belongs to another class. We have the case of the King of Serbia. His Majesty King Edward for two years and more refused to have any dealings with him because he had slain the monarch who sat on the throne of Serbia before him. Yet we are friends of Serbia. We honour King Peter; we respect him; we call Serbia our Ally; we co-operate with the Serbians, yet if the monarch in Russia has been assassinated, or something had happened, we refuse to join hands with the people of Russia on that account. Why? Because in the Serbian Revolution class interest was topmost. In the Russian Revolution the mass interest came topmost. I do not for a, moment suggest that any of us in this House are purposely and consciously behaving in a dishonest manner. But the unfortunate part of every human life is that we are unconsciously the victims of many suppressed prejudices which are inborn in us and are traditional. Now we are face to face with a situation in this world in which, if we are not determined to burst out of these time-worn prejudices and boldly take a new place, if we are not prepared to push forward not only the good but the rights – even the sentimental rights – of the masses of humanity, into the forefront, and if the traditions, the family interests, the class privileges, the profits and dividends of private enterprise, are not set in the background, then neither this Ministry nor any other Ministry will cure the evil, though they may deliver as many speeches as they please, upon it.

21

'DEBATE ON THE ADDRESS'

Margaret Bondfield

Source: House of Commons, 21 January 1924

I feel I must apologise for intervening in this battle of the giants. I am certainly suffering under the depression of the funeral dirge on the right hon. Member for Paisley (Mr. Asquith), to which we have just listened. The points on which I wish to address this House have very little to do with these intellectual scintillations, but they have a great deal to do with the suffering that is going on in this country at the present time amongst unemployed women. Unemployment amongst women, I recognise, is only a small part of a very large problem, but at the same time those of us who have to face these unemployed women day after day realise that for the unemployed women it is the most vital question before the country, and my criticism of the Government is, that in this small problem there was much that could have been done to mitigate the lot of the women, with very little expense, but with a certain amount of administrative common sense, and they have consistently refused to do that little. We have round about a quarter of a million women who have been unemployed during the last three years. The number has varied from time to time, but some of them have been almost continuously unemployed. There were things that could have been done, extensions of schemes that were already in operation, but what is the record of the Government? In 1921, by dint of great pressure from the Central Committee on Women's Employment, backed up by the Trade Union Congress and by large bodies of entirely nonpolitical public opinion, we succeeded in getting a grant of £50,000 allocated to the Central Committee. In 1922 we secured, after tremendous pressure and agitation which ought to have been entirely unnecessary, another grant of £50,000. At the end of December the Central Committee had spent, from the funds at its disposal, £150,000.

The first £50,000 from the Government was conditional on the Central Committee providing £2 to every £1 of the Government. The second was conditional upon the Central Committee putting £1 to every £1 of the Government. With the united fund we have succeeded in passing through various classes about 15,500 people. There are at present not more than 1,000 persons in the training classes, and the last returns show that there are still 250,000 unemployed women, many of whom are again facing a black winter. These small grants were given conditional upon certain training schemes being confined entirely to the development and supply of domestic servants. I am not quarrelling with the necessity for securing domestic work training. I heartily welcome the Report published by the Committee of Inquiry into the conditions of domestic service. It is a sane and practical Report, which has faced facts and realised that there is a curious psychological situation that has to be met, as well as merely a shortage of labour. The recommendations in the Report show a grasp of the whole problem which I hope a future Government will take into account. But the Central Committee could have enormously extended the classes for what we call the home makers. We were not permitted to have any money at all for that category, which would have been so helpful in great areas like Lancashire and Nottingham, Cradley Heath and elsewhere. We have had a certain number of classes there, and we have been able to help a certain number of women, but this had to be done entirely out of the funds raised voluntarily and controlled by the Central Committee on Women's Unemployment.

The War made an enormous difference to the position of women in this respect. I do not think hon. Members realise quite what it means to-day, for example, to be in the clothing trades, compared with what it was 15 years ago. In the clothing trades mass production has developed enormously, and the War accentuated that development. Power machines are the rule rather than the exception, and the specialisation of processes has gone on to such an extent that women who have devoted years to the clothing trade are now in the position of having an option of doing only a thirtieth or even an eightieth part of a garment, and they are kept at that task. Here is a great avenue for helpfulness. The unemployed women in the clothing trade could have been helped by the immediate development of technical classes under the education authorities, where they could learn at least to be able to visualise the processes of a whole garment, and go back to the labour market with knowledge of more than one of the 80 or more processes in the making-up of clothes. That would strengthen the efficiency of the labour supply in the clothing trades and would be an enormous advantage not only to the individual but to the general efficiency of the clothing trade as a whole.

There are other categories of workers in regard to whom there is room for Government action. There are the women in clerical work, many of whom were brought into Government Departments during the War. Of necessity – I do not complain – vast numbers of women were put to do work of a certain elementary kind that did not give them the necessary training or experience to enable them to continue clerical work at the end of the War. These women, above all others, require opportunities for developing technical and general knowledge. In their case classes could have been formed at very little cost. Such classes would have helped to keep up the morale and strengthen the efficiency of the women.

Above all, probably, criticism ought to be directed against the Government administration in regard to their handling of the juvenile question. Boys and girls alike have been at the mercy of a world into which they were turned out of the schools with no place in industry ready to receive them. On boys and girls in the most formative years of their lives, when their characters were influenced by environment, that could have nothing but a disintegrating and deteriorating effect.

Here, too, with a little co-ordination between the Ministry of Labour and the Ministry of Education and any other Department that could have been useful in the matter, surely it might have been possible to build up, not merely an enormous extension of continuation class work, but some opportunities might have been given to the cleverer amongst the children to qualify for better and more extended opportunities of service to the State. We feel that the absence of any co-ordinated effort to deal with juvenile unemployment will go down as one of the gravest marks against the administration of the Government.

I must say a word with regard to inspection. It is very important that we should make laws and that those laws should be good, but they are useless if they are not administered properly. In connection with the legislation that has grown up in the 20th century, inspection has been a vital part of the completion of the law. Take the whole of the ramifications under the Trade Boards Act. The underlying principle enabled the organised workers to work with the organised employers and to get something like a basic rate, filling in the morass of the sweated industries, and getting some sort of firm foundation on which afterwards, by united action, the workers could be maintained and the standard of life raised. We had many employers who welcomed the coming of the Trade Boards, because they recognised that those who desired to deal justly with their people were being saved from a particularly mean and unfair kind of competition. But the success of the Trade Boards depends upon the enforcement of their awards and the enforcement is the business of the inspectors. What has happened in the Trade Board's Department? We had given to the Cave Commission again and again evidence from the Department itself that the staff of inspectors was totally inadequate to deal with the vast problems connected with Trade Board inspection.

We had the humiliating situation last year, when there was a flagrant case of violation in connection with the Tailoring Trade Board rate. It was not the fault of the inspectors, but the Government Department decided that the thing was too difficult, and that it was not possible to conduct a prosecution if they had to deal with a log rate. So the union took up the matter instead. The union won and got an award. It was proved beyond a doubt that it was possible to estimate whether or not the workers were receiving less than the Trade Board's rate. The mischief of the lack of inspection lies in the steady undermining of respect for the law, when that law has been entered into both by employers and workers. These protective laws are in the interests, not merely of the individual concerned, but of the whole community. If we are to advance, we want more of that kind of legislation, but we must insist that when we have got it it shall be fully operative. We want, therefore, a very large extension of the inspectorate.

Is it not ironical that in the very year when factory inspection is the subject of international inquiry, when the Government sends its representatives to Geneva to consider recommendations and covenants laying down the basis of an international system of factory inspection, at a time when the whole world has had its attention directed to the British system of factory inspection – many of us are proud of the record which our inspectors have laid down, for it is a fine tradition, and I had the opportunity in Geneva of meeting inspectors from different countries of the world, and they explained that they were anxious to follow the British method and to develop the British system in their respective countries – is it not ironical that in the year when this has happened, we find a niggardly policy adopted by the Government, which has crippled, hampered, and brought sometimes into disrepute the very system of which we should be so proud? It is a matter of deep regret that these administrative details have been allowed to escape the attention of the Government, because it did not feel the importance of the matter. That is one reason why I am very glad that hon. Members on this side of the House are going to take office. It is not a matter of statistics or of dialectics, but of safeguarding what has been won by tremendous effort and sacrifice on the part of those who are dead and gone.

If I am not regarded as impertinent in the first weeks of my membership of this House, I would say that the speech of the hon. Member for Barrow (Mr. D G. Somerville) brought vividly to my mind a conversation that I had after the 1922 Election with the right hon. Gentleman who lately represented Northampton. He said that for him an election was a mental rest cure. I am bound to say, after the speech of the hon. Member for Barrow, that I felt that his mental rest cure had not yet been completed. I am astounded that the right hon. Gentleman who last addressed the House should still imagine that the country has rejected Socialism. I am a Socialist of 30 years' standing and to-day am a more convinced Socialist than ever I was. Every General Election appears to bring out a larger assortment of entirely imaginary evils, based upon entirely imaginary facts, produced by Members of the party opposite.

It is surely time that we should have perfectly clear-cut divisions – here I echo very cordially the sentiments expressed by the hon. Member for the English Universities (Sir M. Conway) – with regard to intellectual differences. Goodness me! There will always be enough of them to keep us busy and alive and to provide a subject for debate in the House of Commons. There are and will be fundamental differences. Why, then, let us waste the time of the country and of the House by discussing things that have no reality, discussing possible evils that nobody really believes will ever come to pass. Let us get right down to the fundamental differences between those who believe that certain industries will be better under public control than under private control, and those who will not believe that that can ever come. That is a real difference, an understandable difference, an intelligible difference, and I am quite sure the country is debating that difference.

22

'HOUSING (REVISION OF CONTRIBUTIONS) BILL'

Eleanor Rathbone

Source: House of Commons, 22 July 1929

I claim the indulgence which this House always extends to a Member who addresses it for the first time, but I cannot claim indulgence as a novice on the housing question. For the past 19 years I have been a member of the Housing Committee of the Liverpool City Council, one of the local authorities which has been, I think, most active in the matter of housing both before and since the War. In that way, I have had considerable opportunities of observing the effect of the various changes in Parliamentary policy on the action of the local authorities which have been controlled and guided by Parliament. The present Debate is limited to the question of whether His Majesty's Government are right in continuing the subsidy at the present level. I have noticed that practically the whole of the Debate that has taken place has turned upon the question of the effect of the subsidy in two respects. First, on the cost of building, and secondly, on the number of houses that are built with the aid of the subsidy. Upon those two questions I will not intervene, but surely there is another factor which affects the question of whether we want the continuation of the present subsidy, which so far has hardly been touched upon. That is the question whether this subsidy will assist in the production of houses which will meet the need of those who cannot pay economic rents. After all we do not pay subsidies for the sake of houses. We pay subsidies for the sake of tenants, and not for all tenants, but for those who are incapable, without the aid of the subsidy, of providing suitable housing accommodation for themselves. If there were not such tenants we should still need a housing policy for town planning purposes, but we should not need housing subsidies.

Practically every speaker has assumed that the whole question, or almost the whole question, is to secure a continued, and, if possible, a steady supply of that admirable type of houses with which we have all become so familiar – those three-bedroom houses, with or without parlour, with their little gardens fore and aft, which are spreading themselves round every industrial centre in a broad zone, like a sort of milky way, houses that are a refreshing contrast to the dingy rows of brick boxes, with slated lids in which the great majority of the wage earners have hitherto been compelled to be housed. I agree that we do need a practically unlimited supply of those houses, but I agree with one proviso, namely, not at present rents. The question of rents is vital because it determines who will benefit from the houses, whether the houses will benefit those suffering from the housing shortage most acutely and suffering from it longest, and least by their own fault. The question of whether such persons can enter the new houses depends upon the rents at which the houses will be rated. The rents at present vary according to the type of the houses, according to the variations in building costs of the locality and according to the variations in rating in the locality, from about 8s. to 24s., or even more in London. But for the three-bedroom, kitchen house, which we all recognise as the most needed type of house, I believe the average rent, taking the country over, is about 13s. The Housing and Town Planning Association have recently calculated as one result of rather an exhaustive consideration that the cost of that type of house might be reduced to a minimum of something like £400, and that at that price, with the aid of the subsidy and with rates averaging 40 per cent., it could be let for 11s. But there seems no prospect of a reduction either in minimum cost below £400 or in rent below 11s.

The point I want to impress upon the House is that houses at 13s. or even at 11s. are not going to meet the really acute housing need. Who feels that need? Surely those who are at present living either in overcrowded houses or in structurally insanitary houses. Is our present policy doing anything at all appreciable to relieve the need of those two classes – the dwellers in the overcrowded and the structurally insanitary houses? The hon. Member for Withington (Mr. Simon), who spoke the other day in the Debate, has recently produced an admirable little book, which, I hope, everyone interested in the housing problem will read, called "How to abolish the slums." The hon. Member for Withington has shown himself an enthusiastic advocate of subsidies, and of this particular subsidy, and yet the very words with which he began this book are: We have built over 1,000,000 houses since the War. We are well on the way to solving the housing problem so far as the clerk and the artisan are concerned, but we have done nothing for the poorer workers. The condition of the slums in which they are forced to live is probably worse to-day than it was at the end of the War. The overcrowding is almost certainly no better, and the condition of houses is now certainly much worse. That startling statement cannot statistically be proved until the census of 1931 is to hand. I do not think anybody who has practical experience of the housing problem in great cities will doubt its truth. I have not forgotten that the present Bill does not pretend to contain the complete housing policy of the Ministry, especially its policy with regard to slum clearance. We must wait for that until the autumn, but before accepting a Bill the object of which is to keep on the subsidy at the present rate – and, as the right hon. Member for Penryn and Falmouth (Sir J. Tudor Walters) said, there is no indication that the autumn Bill is intended to raise the subsidy – we are surely entitled to ask, whom are we supplying? Otherwise, when the Slum Clearance Bill makes its appearance and when some of us propose Amendments and extensions to that Bill, we may be told: "That would be very nice, but the country cannot afford it." We shall find that we have spent so much money on the slighter and less pressing needs that there is none left for those who need houses the most. It is no use clearing away slums if there are no houses provided at rents within the capacity of the slum dwellers. It has been said that this is only a small Bill. It will only prove small if it fails in its object of increasing the supply of houses. The Financial Memorandum estimates that if 100,000 houses are built in a year under the Bill the additional cost will be £150,000, but, as the Parliamentary Secretary pointed out in reply to the hon. Member for Withington, that is a mere arithmetical platitude. The Bill concerns a difference in the amount of housing subsidy of 30s. per house. Therefore, if 100,000 houses are built in a year, the extra cost will be £150,000, and if 200,000 are built in a year the cost will be £300,000. That is the direct cost. In considering the real extra cost which the Bill is going to place upon the Exchequer, we must add the capitalised value of £6 per annum for 40 years, multiplied by the number of houses that would not have been built if the Bill had not been passed. As no one can compute that, it is easy to represent it as a small Bill.

I am not opposing the Bill, but I would ask whether a Government which represents the party which considers itself specially the party of the under-dog cannot take some steps to secure that the money that we are providing through this Bill and through previous Bills, or at least some portion of it, shall benefit those lower paid workers who cannot afford the present rents? It is quite possible to do that under present legislation, through administrative regulations and through the influence of the local authorities. The crux of the matter is that the local authorities have assumed that because the subsidy is placed on the house, so much per house, it necessarily follows that the subsidy adheres to the house and must be used to lower the rental of the house by a flat rate amount equivalent to the amount of the subsidy. If the object of the subsidy is to provide for those who cannot pay an economic rent, it ignores the fact that capacity or incapacity to pay an economic rent is a personal factor, which does not adhere to the house but adheres to the tenant. Moreover this factor varies in the tenants. It is not merely a question of the prudent people who are going to be housed, or whether they are slum dwellers, or whether a proportion of the houses are in a particular locality, but what is the occupation of the people who are housed and what are their wages . . .

I make a suggestion which is not irrelevant to the purpose of the Bill? It has been repeatedly pointed out that this is a marking-time Bill, to give the Ministry time to consider and bring forward their bigger schemes. Is not the House justified in suggesting that they should be allowed to consider the policy of the future with His Majesty's Government, through a Select Committee? We have had ample evidence from this Debate that the ex-Minister of Health and the ex-Parliamentary Secretary to the Ministry of Health and the present Minister of Health and the present Parliamentary Secretary to the Ministry of Health, have arrived at precisely opposite conclusions as to the effect of the subsidy on the cost of building and the supply of houses. Presumably, they have had precisely the same data to consider. Why may not the House bring its collective wisdom to bear upon the same problem and have an opportunity of considering the data, not merely with a view to determining the effect of the subsidy on the supply and cost of houses, but the much larger question of the effect of the subsidy on the kind of rentals and the kind of tenants; the practicability of the slum clearance scheme, which will be useless unless we have houses in which the dispossessed people can be put; the limits of the possibility of reconditioning, to which ex-Ministers are known to attach much greater practical importance than many of us who have been long thinking of that method believe it will have; the possible effect of the Kent Restriction Acts upon the housing problem, and also the effects of transport facilities upon the housing problem?

During the closing years of the War, I think there were nine committees appointed to discuss various aspects of the housing problem, but they were nearly all of them content to consider the structural aspects of the housing problem, the cost of building, the type of houses, building materials, labour supply and so forth. Now, after the lapse of 10 years, I suggest that we want a Select Committee to consider the housing problem from the tenancy side, to see how we can manage to put up enough houses and to see that those houses pass into the hands of those whose housing needs are the sorest. At present our housing policy may be compared to our having built, at vast cost, a reservoir intended to relieve the thirst of people who are dying of thirst, and then allowing the first call on the water to go to those who need water only for the watering of their roses.

I thank the House for the patience with which it has listened to me, and I am glad that the first occasion on which I have had the opportunity of addressing the House has enabled me to express an opinion which, whether it be a right opinion or a wrong opinion, is the fruits of nearly 20 years of theoretical and practical study of the housing problem, and which has led me to the conclusion that while our study of the housing problem for 20 years, even our pre-War housing problem, has been honestly and painstakingly applied, and has done much good, it has done far less good than it might have done, because it has been vitiated from the first by the economic fallacy that, when you are dealing with a State benefit, which is certainly limited to a comparatively small number of people, because you cannot subsidise houses for the whole population, you can best use that subsidy by a flat-rate reduction of cost; all-round. The problem of incapacity to pay an economic rent is a personal problem and can never be solved, whatever the subsidy may be, by so mechanical a device as a flat-rate arithmetical equal reduction of rent by the amount of the subsidy upon the houses built by the local authorities.

23

'ANNUAL HOLIDAY BILL'

Marion Phillips

Source: House of Commons, 15 November 1929

In listening to the hon. Member for Lowestoft (Sir G. Rentoul), we have been listening almost entirely to points which can be raised on the Committee stage of this Bill. They are not directed to the principle of an annual holiday with payment, but are points of detail as to the way in which that principle shall be carried out. Hon. Members who have opposed this Bill have opposed it very largely on the ground that it is something new, and have then gone on to say that it will disturb collective arrangements which are already in operation and which are successful. I suggest that the ordinary procedure largely followed in this country in industrial legislation is that, first, some agreement is come to between employers and employed, and that later that agreement is extended by law to all employers in all industries. That is the ordinary precedent, which is being followed in this Bill.

As to the suggestion that this is a new principle, I would recall to hon. Members that it has been widely and often discussed, and I would specially remind them of the work of the Reconstruction Committee, appointed in a fit of audacity by the right hon. Member for Carnarvon Boroughs (Mr. Lloyd George), which afterwards became the Reconstruction Ministry. That Committee appointed a Sub-Committee to deal with the problem of the demobilisation of civil war workers, and one of the proposals discussed was to give a holiday with pay to all who had been engaged in munition work. Unfortunately, the Committee could not come to an agreement on that proposal. One section of the Committee thought it would be practicable and right to do so, but they were in a minority. Among them were five Members, including my self, who now sit on the Benches on this side of the House. The other Members of the Committee considered that it was impracticable to give a holiday with pay to munition workers alone, but so struck were all of them with the principle that all workers should have a holiday with pay that, though it was actually outside their terms of reference, they did refer to it, and put that point before the Minister as one on which legislation might take place. I have in my hand the Report of the majority, who included such distinguished people as Mr. H. P. Butler, now Deputy-Director of the International Labour Office, and such well-known employers as Mr. Marchbanks, Mr. Jardine and Mr. Lister. Above their signatures occurs this paragraph: Although it may not be possible to prove it by statistics, we have no doubt that much of the present industrial unrest is due to the mental and physical strain which is being placed not only on munition workers, but, to a greater or lesser extent, on every class of the community owing to the conditions of the war. We think, therefore, that the whole question of holidays might well be considered by the Government as a general measure for the improvement of industrial conditions. This Bill is a general Measure for a holiday with pay as part of the normal industrial conditions – the suggestion which was made by this Committee in April, 1918. The quotation I have read is not from the minority Report, but from the Report of the majority, who are very largely employers and high officials in Government service.

There is one other aspect of this question on which little stress has been laid in the debate to-day, and that is the aspect which it presents to a large class of the community who have a very important job of business management. I refer to the vast army of women who manage the homes of the workers. To the housewife there is always something calamitous in the approach of holidays, because for a very large number of people that means the automatic stopping of wages. An hon. Member opposite gave us a lecture on economics, I hope not economics as taught in the University of London, because as a Member of that university I should be sorry to think that he had learned quite such old fashioned and worn out doctrines in that university during recent years. I listened to him with some surprise when he spoke of the universal workers' holiday in the North of England.

I represent a constituency in the north-east of England, and I will undertake to say that it is a minority of workers in that city that get a holiday, with or without pay. The sort of holiday that my constituents in Sunderland get is an involuntary holiday, with either Poor Law relief, unemployment benefit, or nothing at all. I believe that nothing would come as a more blessed gift to the people in many of our industrial areas, and especially the women, than the fact that they would have a right, after 12 months' work, to a holiday with money with which to pay their way during that holiday. It is quite true that it might have the effect that workers would not try to deny themselves so many pleasures during the year in order to save up for a few days' holiday when it came. It might have that effect, but I think it is doubtful, because I think that, if you give people the certainty of a holiday with a little money coming in during that week, they will be all the more eager to make a good thing of it and have something there to make the time thoroughly enjoyable. I do think, however, that a very large number of the families of the workers have no margin on which they can safely and reasonably afford to save.

If some of us who have been accustomed all our lives to a regular summer holiday, without having to go without wages during that period, would remember how often we came back from our holiday having very badly overspent, and in what difficulties many of us would be if we did not happen to have credit somewhere, we shall realise what a poor thing it is for the great mass of workers to get their holiday and be compelled to run into debt even to supply themselves with their ordinary everyday needs during that time. Even putting out of the question altogether the possibility of going somewhere for enjoyment and recreation, they are in debt at the end of their holiday, because they have no chance of making anything during that time. I am referring here to workers who are allowed to take a little time off but are not allowed to have anything during that period in the way of wages. I do beg this House to think of that mood of generosity which swept over the country at the time when those Reconstruction Committees of which I was speaking were sitting – to get back to the spirit of that period and to say that, since this principle is a good principle, as I think that everybody has admitted who has spoken to-day, we should give a Second Reading to the Bill, and then, when the Bill is in the Committee stage, deal with the difficulties with the intention and the desire to overcome them.

Part 4

RIGHTS AND FREEDOMS

24

'RELIGIOUS LIBERTY'

Charles James Fox

Source: House of Commons, 8 May 1789

The first question which naturally presents itself is, whether the Church and the Constitution are necessarily connected and dependent on each other, and in what degree? And, on this point, I trust the House will be careful how they assent to the proposition of the noble Lord [Lord North]. For my part, I shall not scruple most unequivocally to declare that I conceive that religion should always be distinct from civil government and that it is not otherwise connected with it than as it tends to promote morality among the people, and thus conduces to good order in the State. No human Government has a right to inquire into private opinions, to presume that it knows them, or to act on that presumption. Men are the best judges of the consequences of their own opinions, and how far they are likely to influence their actions; and it is most unnatural and tyrannical to say, 'As you think, so you must act. I will collect the evidence of your future conduct from what I know to be your opinions'. The very reverse of this is the rule of conduct which ought to be pursued. Men ought to be judged by their actions, and not by their thoughts. The one can be fixed and ascertained, the other can only be a matter of speculation. So far am I of this opinion that, if any man publishes his political sentiments, and says in writing that he dislikes the Constitution of this country, and gives it as his judgment that principles in direct contradiction to the Constitution and Government are the principles which ought to be asserted and maintained, such an author ought not, in my judgment, on that account to be disabled from filling any office, civil or military; but, if he carried his detestable opinions into practice, the law would then find a remedy, and punish him for his conduct, grounded on his opinions, as an example to deter others from acting in the same dangerous and absurd manner.

No proposition can, I contend, prove more consonant to common sense, to reason and to justice, than that men should be tried by their actions and not by their opinions; their actions ought to be waited for, and not guessed at, as the probable consequence of the sentiments which they are known to entertain and to profess. If the reverse of this doctrine was ever adopted as a maxim of government, if the actions of man were to be prejudged from their opinions, it would sow the seeds of jealousy and distrust, it would give scope to private malice, it would sharpen the minds of men against one another, incite each man to divine the private opinions of his neighbour, to deduce mischievous consequences from them, and thence to prove that he ought to incur disabilities, and be fettered with restrictions. This, if true with respect to political, is more peculiarly so with regard to religious opinions; and, from the mischievous principle which I have described, flows every species of party zeal, every system of political intolerance, every extravagance of religious hate.

25

A HABEAS CORPUS SUSPENSION ACT, 1794

Source: *A Habeas Corpus Suspension Act*, 1794, 34 Geo. III, c. 54

'Whereas a traitorous and detestable Conspiracy has been formed for subverting the existing Laws and Constitution, and for introducing the System of Anarchy and Confusion which has so fatally prevailed in *France*:' Therefore, for the better Preservation of his Majesty's sacred Person, and for securing the Peace and the Laws and Liberties of this Kingdom; be it enacted . . . That every Person or Persons that are or shall be in Prison within the Kingdom of *Great Britain* at or upon the Day on which this Act shall receive his Majesty's Royal Assent, or after, by Warrant of his said Majesty's most Honourable Privy Council, signed by six of the said Privy Council, for High Treason, Suspicion of High Treason, or treasonable Practices, or by Warrant, signed by any of his Majesty's Secretaries of State, for such Causes as aforesaid, may be detained in safe Custody, without Bail or Mainprize, until the first Day of *February* one thousand seven hundred and ninety-five; and that no Judge or Justice of the Peace shall bail or try any such Person or Persons so committed, without Order from his said Majesty's Privy Council signed by six of the said Privy Council, till the said first Day of February one thousand seven hundred and ninety-five; any Law or Statute to the contrary notwithstanding.

III. Provided always, and be it enacted, That nothing in this Act shall be construed to extend to invalidate the ancient Rights and Privileges of Parliament, or to the Imprisonment or Detaining of any Member of either House of Parliament during the Sitting of such Parliament, until the Matter of which he stands suspected be first communicated to the House of which he is a Member, and the Consent of the said House obtained for his Commitment or Detaining.

26

'THE CASE OF WOLF TONE'

Source: Thomas Bayly Howell, *A Complete Collection of State Trials and Proceedings for High Treason and Other Crimes and Misdemeanors from the Earliest Period to the Year 1783*, Volume 27, pp. 625–626.

"I do not pretend to say," observed Mr. Curran, "that Mr. Tone is not guilty of the charges of which he was accused; – I presume the officers were honourable men; – but it is stated in the affidavit, as a solemn fact, that Mr. Tone had no commission under His Majesty, and therefore no court martial could have any cognizance of any crime imputed to him, while the Court of King's Bench sat in the capacity of the great criminal court of the land. In times when war was raging, when man was opposed to man in the field, courts martial might be endured; but every law authority is with me, while I stand upon this sacred and immutable principle of the constitution – *that martial law and civil law are incompatible*; and that the former must cease with the existence of the latter. This is not the time for arguing this momentous question. My client must appear in this court. *He is cast for death this day*. He may be ordered for execution while I address you. I call on the Court to support the law.[1] I move for a *habeas corpus* to be directed to the provost marshal of the barracks of Dublin, and major Sandys to bring up the body of Mr. Tone.

Lord Chief Justice [Kilwarden]. – Have a writ instantly prepared.

Mr. *Curran*. – My client may die while this writ is preparing.

Lord Chief Justice. – Mr. Sheriff, proceed to the barracks, and acquaint the provost-marshal that a writ is preparing to suspend Mr. Tone's execution; and *see that he be not executed*.

[The Court awaited in a state of the utmost agitation, the return of the Sheriff.]

Mr. *Sheriff*. – My lords, I have been at the barracks, in pursuance of your order. The provost-marshal says he must obey major Sandys. Major Sandys says he must obey lord Cornwallis.

Mr. *Curran*. – Mr. Tone's father, my lords, returns, after serving the Habeas Corpus: he says general Craig will not obey it.

Lord Chief Justice. – Mr. Sheriff, take the body of Tone into your custody. Take the provost-marshal and major Sandys into custody: and show the order of this Court to general Craig.

Mr. *Sheriff* (who was understood to have been refused admittance at the barracks) returns. – I have been at the barracks. Mr. Tone, having cut his throat last night, is not in a condition to be removed. As to the second part of your order, I could not meet the parties.

[A French Emigrant Surgeon, whom General Craig had sent along with the Sheriff, was sworn.]

Surgeon. – I was sent to attend Mr. Tone this morning at four o'clock, his windpipe was divided. I took instant measures to secure his life, by closing the wound. There is no knowing, for four days, whether it will be mortal. His head is now kept in one position. *A sentinel is over him, to prevent his speaking.* His removal would kill him.

Mr. Curran applied for further surgical aid, and for the admission of Mr. Tone's friends to him. [*Refused.*]

Lord Chief Justice. – Let a rule be made for suspending the execution of Theobald Wolfe Tone; and let it be served on the proper persons.

27

COMBINATION ACT, 1800

Source: *Combination Act*, 1800, 39 Geo. III, c. 81

Whereas it is expedient to explain and amend an Act . . . to prevent unlawful combinations of workmen . . . be it enacted . . . that from . . . the passing of this Act . . . all contracts, covenants and agreements whatsoever . . . at any time . . . heretofore made . . . between any journeymen manufacturers or other persons . . . for obtaining an advance of wages of them or any of them, or any other journeymen manufacturers or workmen, or other persons in any manufacture, trade or business, or for lessening or altering their or any of their usual hours or nine of working, or for decreasing the quantity of work (save and except any contract made or to be made between any master and his journeyman or manufacturer, for or on account of the work or service of such journeyman or manufacturer with whom such contract may be made), or for preventing or hindering any person or persons from employing whomsoever he, she, or they shall think proper to employ . . . or for controlling or anyway affecting any person or persons carrying on any manufacture, trade or business, in the conduct or management thereof, shall be . . . illegal, null and void. . . .

No journeyman, workman or other person shall at any time after the passing of this Act make or enter into, or be concerned in the making of or entering into any such contract, covenant or agreement, in writing or not in writing . . . and every . . . workman . . . who, after the passing of this Act, shall be guilty of any of the said offences, being thereof lawfully convicted, upon his own confession, or the oath or oaths of one or more credible witness or witnesses, before any two justices of the Peace . . . within three calendar months next after the offence shall have been committed, shall, by order of such justices, be committed to and confined in the common gaol, within his or their jurisdiction, for any time not exceeding 3 calendar months, or at the discretion of such justices shall be committed to some House of Correction within the same jurisdiction, there to remain and to be kept to hard labour for any time not exceeding 2 calendar months . . .

Every . . . workman . . . who shall at any time after the passing of this Act enter into any combination to obtain an advance of wages, or to lessen or alter the hours or duration of the time of working, or to decrease the quantity of work, or for any other purpose contrary to this Act, or who shall, by giving money, or by persuasion, solicitation or intimidation, or any other means, wilfully and maliciously endeavour to prevent any unhired or unemployed journeyman or workman, or other person, in any manufacture, trade or business, or any other person wanting employment in such manufacture, trade or business, from hiring himself to any manufacturer or tradesman, or person conducting any manufacture, trade or business, or who shall, for the purpose of obtaining an advance of wages, or for any other purpose contrary to the provisions of this Act, wilfully and maliciously decoy, persuade, solicit, intimidate, influence or prevail, or attempt or endeavour to prevail, on any journeyman or workman, or other person hired or employed, or to be hired or employed in any such manufacture, trade or business, to quit or leave his work, service or employment, or who shall wilfully and maliciously hinder or prevent any manufacturer or tradesman, or other person, from employing in his or her manufacture, trade or business, such journeymen, workmen and other persons as he or she shall think proper, or who, being hired or employed, shall, without any just or reasonable cause, refuse to work with any other journeyman or workman employed or hired to work therein, and who shall be lawfully convicted of any of the said offences, upon his own confession, or the oath or oaths of one or more credible witness or witnesses, before any two justices of the Peace for the county. . . . or place where such offence shall be committed, within 3 calendar months . . . shall, by order of such justices, be committed to . . . gaol for any time not exceeding 3 calendar months; or otherwise be committed to some House of Correction . . . for any time not exceeding 2 calendar months . . .

And for the more effectual suppression of all combinations amongst journeymen, workmen and other persons employed in any manufacture, trade or business, be it further enacted, that all and every persons and person whomsoever (whether employed in any such manufacture, trade or business, or not) who shall attend any meeting had or held for the purpose of making or entering into any contract, covenant or agreement, by this Act declared to be illegal, or of entering into, supporting, maintaining, continuing, or carrying on any combination for any purpose by this Act declared to be illegal, or who shall summons, give notice to, call upon, persuade, entice, solicit, or by intimidation, or any other means, endeavour to induce any journeyman, workman, or other person, employed in any manufacture, trade or business, to attend any such meeting, or who shall collect, demand, ask, or receive any sum of money from any such journeyman, workman, or other person, for any of the purposes aforesaid, or who shall persuade, entice, solicit, or by intimidation, or any other means, endeavour to induce any such journeyman, workman or other person to enter into or be concerned in any such combination, or who shall pay any sum of money, or make or enter into any subscription or contribution, for or towards the support or encouragement of any such illegal meeting or combination, and who shall be lawfully convicted of any of the said offences, upon his own confession, or the oath or oaths of one or more credible witness or witnesses, before any two justices of the Peace. . . . within 3 calendar months . . . shall . . . be committed to and confined in the common gaol . . . for any time not exceeding 3 calendar months, or otherwise be committed to some House of Correction. . . . . . . for any time not exceeding 2 calendar months . . .

And whereas it will be a great convenience and advantage to masters and workmen engaged in manufactures, that a cheap and summary mode be established for settling all disputes that may arise between them respecting wages and work; be it further enacted . . . that, from and after 1 August . . . 1800, in all cases that shall or may arise within . . . England, where the masters and workmen cannot agree respecting the price or prices to be paid for work actually done in any manufacture, or any injury or damage done or alleged to have been done by the workmen to the work, or respecting any delay or supposed delay on the part of the workmen in finishing the work, or the not finishing such work in a good and workman-like manner, or according to any contract; and in all cases of dispute or difference, touching any contract or agreement for work or wages between masters and workmen in any trade or manufacture, which cannot be otherwise mutually adjusted and settled by and between them, it shall and may be, and it is hereby declared to be lawful for such masters and workmen between whom such dispute or difference shall arise . . . or either of them, to demand and have an arbitration or reference of such matter or matters in dispute; and each of them is hereby authorised and empowered forthwith to nominate and appoint an arbitrator . . . to arbitrate and determine such matter or matters in dispute as aforesaid by writing, subscribed by him in the presence of and attested by one witness . . . and to deliver the same personally to the other party . . . and to require the other party to name an arbitrator in like manner within two days after such reference to arbitration shall have been so demanded; and such arbitrators so appointed . . . are hereby authorised and required to . . . examine upon oath the parties and their witnesses . . . and forthwith to proceed to hear and determine the complaints of the parties, and the matter or matters in dispute between them; and the award to be made by such arbitrators within the time herein-after limited, shall in all cases be final and conclusive between the parties; but in case such arbitrators so appointed shall not agree to decide such matter or matters in dispute, so to be referred to them as aforesaid, and shall not make and sign their award within the space of three days after the signing of the submission to their award by both parties, that then it shall be lawful for the parties or either of them to require such arbitrators forthwith and without delay to go before and attend upon one of his Majesty's justices of the Peace acting in and for the county . . . or place where such dispute shall happen and be referred, and state to such justice the points in difference between them . . . which points . . . the said justice shall . . . hear and determine, and for that purpose . . . examine the parties and their witnesses upon oath, if he shall think fit. . . .

28

'STANDING ORDER FOR THE EXCLUSION OF STRANGERS'

Richard Sheridan

Source: House of Commons, 6 February 1810

Mr. Sheridan rose to submit the proposition to the House, of which he had on the last evening given notice; and although he felt it to be a subject of the greatest importance, he still could not coincide in the apprehensions of those who considered this interference with what was called the Standing Order of that House, as a matter attended with mighty difficulties and with peculiar delicacy. In delivering his sentiments upon this subject, it was wholly unnecessary for him to take up any considerable portion of their time. Neither did the plain statement to which he should confine himself stand in need of adventitious ornaments. There was little use for calling forth either the cogency of argument, or the decorations of language, to recommend the course which he should propose; for if the good sense of the House, its willingness to stand high in the estimation of the country, and to hold firm the confidence of its constituents – if all such powerful and persuasive inducements could not influence them, then it would be idle to expect that such auxiliary aids could make an impression. There was nothing in what he should propose which savoured of party motive or of political bias; his sole object was to impress upon that House the vital necessity of meriting by its conduct, at this critical period more than ever, the confidence of the people. That being; his view of the question, he could not lend himself to the apprehensions of those who, from most honourable motives he was convinced, had felt it to be their duty to call into action that mistakenly supposed Standing Order for the Exclusion of Strangers. Unwilling as he was to create any irritation in the discussion of this subject, he still must ask, what was there in the present investigation, in which the House was engaged, that called for concealment and secrecy, disclaimed and refused in a recent inquiry, which from its nature might have pleaded for that delicacy – in that inquiry where the House was compelled to tear aside the veil which the imperfections of humanity had thrown over the frailties of domestic life? Shall then the House grant to an accused ministry that protection which concealment can afford, upon a great question of political importance, involving the honour, the interests, and the character of the county, after having refused it to the son of their sovereign, in a case where the very nature and character of the transactions inquired into would have naturally prompted to the temporary suspension of reporting daily its proceedings? He was ready to believe that ministers did not wish to screen their conduct by such an expedient; and even if they did, he was sure, from the independent political career of the right hon. gent. (Mr. Yorke) who had enforced the Order, that he would have disdained to be their instrument for any such purpose. It was not the wish, he was assured, of the two Secretaries of State to have any such course pursued. It had indeed been expressed as the wish of the noble lord (Castlereagh) that the investigation should be as open and public as possible, that the scrutiny into his share of those transactions which were to be the subject of inquiry, should be both strict and rigorous. What, then, could have induced the right hon. gent. to press this Order at this most perilous crisis? What could be the advantage in this House meeting the public hope, by an act which must lead to public disappointment? How can that examination which the country and the House, had proclaimed to be necessary for our honour and security, prove by its publicity through the ordinary channels, to be mischievous to the public interests? From what had fallen from the right hon. gent. (Mr. Yorke), it might be inferred that he was apprehensive lest a partial or garbled publication of the evidence might be made by the daily prints. But he must be allowed to observe, that, in the communication of the transactions of that House, the editors of the Public Journals had been uniformly guided by the strictest impartiality. There never was exerted any undue influence, never felt any improper bias in giving parliamentary reports. But if there was one point upon which they were more scrupulous than another relative to the proceedings of that House, it was in correctly and fully communicating the details of evidence when examined at the bar. Were even the editors inclined from motives of their own, or corrupt views of self interest, to excite any improper prejudice by mutilated or unjustifiable statements, he was confident that not one of the gentlemen who were in the habit of taking the reports of that House, would lend himself to such an improper service. Suppose they should not choose to make correct reports of what passed in that House, would it be endured by the country? Would any one purchase their papers which did not give so material a feature of intelligence? Why then preclude them from this particular subject of investigation? But the right hon. gent. (Mr. Yorke) had stated that the newspapers could take copies of the Minutes printed by the order of the House. They certainly can, but it was wholly at their option; and will it be endured that the country should be deprived of that information which it is most alive to be possessed of, that it should be kept in complete ignorance of what parliament was doing at one of the most awful moments of its existence; for surely it would not be contended that the papers printed by the order of that House could by any possibility circulate throughout the mass of the population of these kingdoms? But even were these documents to circulate, they would only convey the mere questions and answers. All the interlocutory discussion would be suppressed, and perhaps questions of the most vital importance for ever withheld from the knowledge of the people. He would put an instance – had it not occurred when with shut doors they were engaged in debate on a former night, that the whole inquisitorial power of the House of Commons was made questionable? When it was contended by the minister of England, that it had not the power to demand answers from a witness at its bar, because he was a privy counsellor. It was true, that the right hon. gent. who had then thrown down the gauntlet, had since receded from the contest; yet still he would ask, whether upon an interlocutory discussion of this kind, involving the character, nay the very constitution of that House in the exercise of the whole of its inquisitorial powers, it was not right that the British people should know who were the members in that House, who would support such a principle, and what were the arguments by which such extraordinary doctrine was upheld? He was assured, that were the House polled upon the propriety of enforcing the order of exclusion, the wish of the majority would be to proceed upon the present question, in a similar manner as it had done with the inquiry last session. If, then, such was the feeling of the House, he would put it to hon. gentlemen, whether it was not most preposterous, that it should be in the power of any individual, either in his wisdom or his caprice, to defeat its general wish, and that upon a question in which the House had not the remotest desire to disgust the public mind, by screening itself under the mask of concealment. – He was perfectly assured that the right hon. gent. who had enforced the standing order, did not act from any impression or suggestion that it would be agreeable to, or was desired by ministers, in order to shelter their conduct, from exposure by the publicity of the investigation. He verily believed he was one of the last men who would lend himself to such a purpose and he was, therefore, greatly surprised at his persisting in a measure which could not fail of being highly repugnant to the feelings of the public, as well as highly injurious to the interests of the nation. It was known to be the universal wish throughout the country, that this inquiry should be carried on in the manner most likely to promote the ends of public justice, and would the nation give credit to that House for a sincere and honest desire to comply with its wishes, if they were to involve their proceedings in mystery and concealment? A House of Commons, that regarded its own character, and respected the opinion of its constituents and the public, should not resist the feelings of the public at a period like the present. He begged to ask what was the sanctity of this supposed Standing Order? In the first place, he must contend that it was no Standing Order at all. – Was it a part of the Lex Parliamentaria, one of those fundamental principles the elements of their existence, interwoven with the constitution of the House itself. It was no such thing, but merely took its place among many other good and many other frivolous regulations, affecting the proceedings of that House. It was passed at the opening of the session, upon question which might have been rejected, when proposed, and, of course, liable to revision, and repeal, on any subsequent occasion. But of all other regulations, the present order had this peculiarity, that the very act of enforcing it defeated its object. It had been his lot to have proved this experiment upon a former occasion, when this system of exclusion was insisted upon by rather an obstinate member. Finding that hon. member still determined to persevere, he had assured him, that if the order were to be in future inforced, it should be fully inforced and strictly executed: that he should have the bond and nothing but the bond. This intimation had its effect, and it was not till the present inquiry that any further attempt had been made to inforce the order. But it was a most mistaken idea to conceive that this order empowered any member to call upon strangers to withdraw. It allowed of no such interference, nor invested any member with such authority. Here the right hon. member read the Order, which says, That any stranger appearing in the House shall be taken into custody by the Serjeant. If the House therefore were determined to enforce the Order, they must do it in the very words, and must direct that all the strangers present be secured; as the Order directly calls upon the Serjeant at Arms to take into actual custody all strangers, without distinction of persons, who shall have intruded themselves into the House. By being present the offence is committed, and any member of the House had no more right to order the culprit who had intruded, to withdraw, than he would have to rescue him after his committal into custody. – The power and authority rested with the Serjeant at Arms alone; and how was he to enforce it? If in proceeding to obey the order the Serjeant should find two or three hundred persons collected in the gallery, it would obviously be impossible for him to take them all into custody, and therefore he must shut them up in the gallery, whilst he went to collect his posse comitatus. But Whilst he is assembling his forces, the debate goes on; the strangers are in possession of all that has passed; and thus, by its very operation, the object of this Standing Order is defeated. But if this Order claims such particular reverence, let it be considered there are many others, which any other member could move to have enforced. For instance, that no footman shall be allowed in the passages leading to this House; and indeed, any member addicted to early rising (a laugh) might, if he were captious, enforce the order for the House meeting at 10 o'clock in the morning. There was also another order, which stated it to be the privilege of members to pass strangers through the House into the gallery, except whilst the House is sitting. Here, then, were two orders wholly irreconcileable, unless it was intended, that the members should introduce their friends, for the purpose of being committed to the custody of the Serjeant at Arms. Was it not, then, a duty to reconcile such orders to themselves, and both to common sense? He did not mean to convey an opinion, or to maintain it as a rule, that there never could arise an occasion when strangers ought to be excluded, but he did wish to have the order so modified that it should not depend upon the caprice or pleasure of any individual member, but should be fairly submitted to the decision of the House: that if any hon. gent. should think proper to inforce the order he should afterwards be called upon to state some reason for his conduct. It would be apparent from this observation, that it was not his intention to move for the repeal of the order: all he wanted was to bring it under the consideration of the House in a constitutional manner. – In the courts of justice, when any particular case excited the public curiosity, the people went in by a rush. God forbid that in the House of Commons the gallery should be filled in this tumultuous manner; but if that should happen to be the case, would the House think of taking into custody those who were introduced by members, and in conformity to an order, reputed a standing order. He thought that where strangers were introduced by members, they should be allowed to continue, except when the question was such that it was not proper to be discussed before strangers. Such a subject had not frequently occurred; and he could not conceive why in the present case it should be deemed necessary to exclude strangers. To permit strangers to hear the discussion on this subject, would be the most likely way to ingratiate the House with the public. They had lately been used to it day after day. When the character of the king's son was to be investigated, and his conduct sifted in the minutest manner, not a syllable had been heard of the exclusion of strangers; but, when the conduct and character of ministers was to be inquired into, then it appeared to be a subject too tender and delicate for public inspection in that House. He thought there never was a period in our history, in which it was more necessary for parliament to conciliate the public; and, wishing that to be the case, he would move, "That a Committee of Privileges be appointed to meet to-morrow, in the Speaker's Chamber, to consider the order Of the 25th of January last."

29

'HABEAS CORPUS SUSPENSION BILL'

Sir Samuel Romilly

Source: House of Commons, 26 February 1817

Sir Samuel Romilly would not long occupy the attention of the House, but he could not prevail upon himself to give a silent vote upon the most important question that had been discussed since he had had a seat in parliament. All parties were agreed upon the inestimable value of that part of the constitution which it was proposed for a time to annul: and there were few that denied that at present great evils existed, and that those evils required a speedy remedy. The question was therefore reduced to a very narrow compass, viz. Was this a case in which it was necessary to have recourse to such a remedy, and was the remedy adapted to the nature of the evils? The first point must depend upon a preliminary question, whether other means had been duly resorted to, and whether those means had failed of success? The noble lord had repeatedly declared, that the utmost vigilance of ministers had been exerted; but it was now quite clear, from subsequent intelligence, that that utmost vigilance, in truth amounted to nothing. It was admitted by the noble lord, that these traitorous designs had been proceeding for a considerable time before the aid of parliament was required; yet, although ministers had been fully apprized of the attempts upon the loyalty, the morals, and the religion of the people; though they had been in possession of the libellous and blasphemous publications so industriously circulated among the lower orders; yet up to the present moment, not a single prosecution had been instituted against the authors. The excuse of the attorney-general for this procrastination was most extraordinary and curious: in truth, he said, the libels laid before him were so numerous, that he could not see where prosecutions were to end. Where they were to end, he (sir S R.) did not pretend to decide; but it was not very difficult to determine where they ought to have begun. The libels might be numerous, but if they were, nothing had been publicly known of them till lately; and the more numerous the more urgent was the necessity that some of the authors should be severely punished, as a terror and an example to the rest. He entreated the House to recur once more to the consideration of all that had occurred, previous to the suspension of the Habeas Corpus act in 1794. Very different then had been the conduct of government, for that measure had not been suggested to the House until after prosecutions had been instituted for sedition at evey quarter sessions in all corners of the kingdom. At that period, at least parliament had not been required to suspend the rights of the subjects of the crown until recourse had been had to the existing laws. He much doubted, indeed, if those laws had not been too severely enforced, some notorious criminals ought to have been selected, instead of the indiscriminate and sweeping punishments awarded against every petty offender. He was surprised to observe the smile of contempt on the face of the hon. and learned gentleman intended as it was to deride the censure of conduct directly opposite to that which he had thought fit to pursue. The learned lord advocate of Scotland, to the surprise and dismay of his friends, had produced an oath taken at Glasgow by some deluded persons, with the existence of which oath it appeared that ministers had been some time acquainted. Were they not aware that the most severe punishment known to the law might be inflicted upon individuals subscribing that oath? Did they not know that it was felony without benefit of clergy, unless the person taking the oath, within 14 days afterwards abandoned his associates, and betrayed their purposes? As to the question, whether this suspension were adapted to the existing evils, the only individual who had contended that it was so, was the hon. member who spoke last: he contended that, as sufficient evidence could not be procured to convict, it was therefore proper to give ministers unlimited power to imprison. As the delinquent could not be brought to trial, he was to be punished without it. On the contrary, he(sir S.R.) contended, that this measure was in no way calculated to meet the evil. Government could fix upon no individual of leading influence or talent, whose arrest would check the progress of disaffection, and defeat the operations of the minor agents: all were alike insignificant, and the extent to which the infection had spread, and was spreading, was the real evil. Would the imprisonment of two or three poor wretches prevent the diffusion of the poison through all the intricate ramifications, by which it was conveyed to the public mind? If indeed they were publicly tried, regularly convicted, and exemplarily punished, something would be gained – others would be deterred, for the fact would be known; but the mere unheard-of confinement of two or three mechanics would effect nothing in stopping the active mischief of particular individuals. In 1794 the state of things was widely different in another respect; then no petitions were presented humbly praying that parliament would reform itself; but a convention existed to serve as a substitute for parliament. In 1799 it was again suspended, but the country was then threatened with invasion; the disaffected then refused to acknowledge any parliament at all, and in its place substituted the National Assembly of France, which boasted of its secret and active correspondence with this country. The object then was not to reform, but to supersede parliament. Much as he censured the adoption of this measure now, he was not one of those who thought that the Habeas Corpus act ought never to be suspended; under some circumstances, the suspension might be most wise and necessary, and those circumstances had existed when, on former occasions, persons of great consequence and influence were in league with an enemy, and when their arrest paralyzed the traitorous designs of all their dependants. But was such the case at present? Where could ministers find one man of influence or consequence among the disaffected of our day? Where could they find even a man of the middle rank of life, among the vulgar, ignorant, and deluded wretches against whom ministers were about to launch their vengeance? How then could this suspension be useful, unless indeed this government followed the example of a state it had recently supported, against the avowed wish of the people, in which not merely obnoxious individuals, but the inhabitants of whole villages and towns, had been thrown into dungeons. Was not this, he confidently demanded, a most powerful reason for refusing what was now required? Would the House intrust ministers with a power by which persons of low rank and obscure occupations, in shoals, would be placed at the mercy of every truckling informer? The noble lord had adverted on a former night to the names of individuals in higher stations, who had been placed by these infatuated reformers upon what they termed the committee of safety or conservative body; but because misguided and illiterate men had had the audacity, without the slightest authority, to place upon this list persons of the most undoubted loyalty and of elevated rank, did it afford such a presumption of guilt as to justify the bold declaration of the noble lord, that in the eyes of God and man they were answerable for all the consequences of rebellion? Undoubtedly, the names of those most respectable persons were found there, on account of the sentiments they were known to entertain; and the noble lord, and a right hon. gentleman after him, had explained the declaration as a caution to certain individuals against supporting popular doctrines; which was as much as to to say, that no man was to argue in favour of parliamentary reform, the liberty of the press, or any other topic displeasing to the other side of the House, unless he wished to fall under the dreadful denunciation of the noble lord. He [sir S. R.] was not fond of making personal allusions, and he was the more unwilling now, because the noble lord had this night shown a remarkable soreness upon some points; but he could not help just observing, that there was a period, even of the noble lord's life, when he might have had the misfortune to fall under his own denunciations, and to have been included in a list of a committee of safety. The liberality of the noble lord's opinions at one time, and the pledges of championship in the cause of parliamentary reform, given by him at an early period of his political life, before he had entered into office, or had been planted in any of the hot-beds or nurseries for young statesmen, might have rendered even him responsible in the eyes of God and man for the consequences of disaffection and rebellion. But the noble lord had got a seat in the cabinet; which put him out of the way of such perils. Reverting more immediately to the question he called upon the House not to withdraw a protection from the lower classes, to which they were as much entitled as the most exalted individual he was then addressing. It was impossible to calculate upon the abuses to which the measure might be subject; and at its expiration the minister would only have to come down to the House with a bill of indemnity, and his responsibility would be at an end. Our ancestors had never consented to the suspension of the Habeas Corpus act but in cases of extreme danger; and the proposal was now the more alarming on account of the precedent it would establish. It was now for the first time laid down, that under any circumstances of alarm the rights of Englishmen were to be dispensed with. Yet, in the years 1767 and 1768, when, according to the letters of Dr. Franklin, great distress, unusual scarcity, and alarming riots prevailed, no person had ever dreamt of suspending the Habeas Corpus act. Now, however, in time of profound peace, it was contended, that the race of Englishmen was so degenerate that they were incapable of their own protection; and in consequence of their weakness and pusillanimity were willing to make a voluntary sacrifice of their dearest rights into the hands of his majesty's ministers. True it was, that dangers threatened the country: but he would ask, was there no danger in empowering a few individuals to imprison all the rest of the subjects of the Crown, and that too without the slightest responsibility? Was there no danger in this suspension, when the standing army was so overgrown, and when already government possessed more influence than it had ever before enjoyed? Was there no danger even to general liberty, when foreign states, already sufficiently disposed to check its growth, should see this once free country placed under the absolute dominion of its ministers on account of the absurd schemes of a few miserable Spenceans? Was there no danger in public opinion, and that even to ministers themselves? Were they well assured that this measure would have, in truth, the effect of strengthening their weak hands? Would not the people see through the artifice of those who, under pretence of public security, were only endeavouring to secure themselves? In every point of view, he thought the suspension objectionable: the dangers might be great, but the existing laws had not yet been tried; and if tried he was convinced that they would be found sufficient for every purpose of national protection.

30

REPEAL OF THE TEST AND CORPORATION ACTS, 1828

Source: *Repeal of the Test and Corporation Acts*, 1828, 9 Geo. IV, c. 17

'Whereas an Act was passed in the Thirteenth Year of the Reign of King *Charles* the Second, intituled *An Act for the well governing and regulating of Corporations*: and Whereas another Act was passed in the Twenty-fifth Year of the Reign of King *Charles* the Second, intituled *An Act for preventing Dangers which may happen from Popish Recusants*: And Whereas another Act was passed in the Sixteenth Year of the Reign of King *George* the Second, intituled *An Act to indemnify Persons who have omitted to qualify themselves for Offices and Employments within the Time limited by Law, and for allowing further Time for that Purpose; and also for amending so much of an Act made in the Twenty-fifth year of the Reign of King Charles the Second, intituled, 'An Act for preventing Dangers which may happen from Popish Recusants' as relates to the Time for receiving the Sacrament of the Lord's Supper now limited by the said Act:* And Whereas it is expedient that so much of the said several Acts of Parliament as imposes the Necessity of taking the Sacrament of the Lord's Supper according to the Rites or Usage of the Church of *England*, for the Purposes therein respectively mentioned, should be repealed:' Be it therefore enacted . . . That so much and such Parts of the said several Acts . . . as require the Person or Persons in the said Acts respectively described to take or receive the Sacrament of the Lord's Supper according to the Rites or Usage of the Church of *England*, for the several Purposes therein expressed, or to deliver a Certificate, or to make Proof of the Truth of such his or their receiving the said Sacrament in manner aforesaid, or as impose upon any such Person or Persons any Penalty, Forfeiture, Incapacity, or Disability whatsoever for or by reason of any Neglect or Omission to take or receive the said Sacrament, within the respective Periods and in the Manner in the said Acts respectively provided in that Behalf, shall, from and immediately after the passing of this Act, be and the same are hereby repealed.

II. 'And Whereas the Protestant Episcopal Church of *England* and *Ireland*, and the Doctrine, Discipline, and Government thereof, and the Protestant Presbyterian Church of *Scotland*, and the Doctrine, Discipline and Government thereof, are by the Laws of this Realm severally established, permanently and inviolably.': . . . Be it therefore enacted, That every Person who shall hereafter be placed, elected, or chosen in or to any Office of Mayor, Alderman, Recorder, Bailiff, Town Clerk, or Common Councilman, or in or to any Office of Magistracy, or Place, Trust, or Employment relating to the Government of any City, Corporation, Borough, or Cinque Port within *England* and *Wales* or the Town of *Berwick-upon-Tweed*, shall, within One Calendar Month next before or upon his Admission into any of the aforesaid Offices or Trusts, make and subscribe the Declaration following:

'I *A. B.* do solemnly and sincerely, in the Presence of God, profess, testify, and declare, upon the true Faith of a Christian, That I will never exercise any Power, Authority or Influence I may possess by virtue of the Office of to injure or weaken the Protestant Church as it is by Law established in *England*, or to disturb the said Church, or the Bishops and Clergy of the said Church, in the Possession of any Rights or Privileges to which such Church, or the said Bishops and Clergy, are or may be by Law entitled.'

III. And be it enacted, That the said Declaration shall be made and subscribed, as aforesaid, in the Presence of such Person or Persons respectively, who, by the Charters or Usages of the said respective Cities, Corporations, Boroughs, and Cinque Ports, ought to administer the Oath for the due Execution of the said Offices or Places respectively, and in default of such, in the Presence of Two Justices of the Peace of the respective Counties, Ridings, Divisions, or Franchises, wherein the said Cities, Corporations, Boroughs, and Cinque Ports are; which said Declaration shall either be entered in a Book, Roll, or other Record, to be kept for that Purpose, or shall be filed amongst the Records of the City, Corporation, Borough or Cinque Port.

IV. And be it enacted, That if any Person, placed, elected, or chosen into any of the aforesaid Offices or Places, shall omit or neglect to make and subscribe the said Declaration in manner above mentioned, such Placing, Election, or Choice shall be void. . . .

V. And be it further enacted, That every Person who shall hereafter be admitted into any Office or Employment, or who shall accept from His Majesty, His Heirs or Successors, any Patent, Grant, or Commission, and who by his Admittance into such Office or Employment or Place of Trust, or by his Acceptance of such Patent, Grant, or Commission, or by the Receipt of any Pay, Salary, Fee, or Wages by reason thereof, would, by the Laws in force immediately before the passing of this Act have been required to take the Sacrament of the Lord's Supper according to the Rites or Usage of the Church of *England*, shall, within Six Calendar Months after his Admission to such Office, Employment, or Place of Trust, or his Acceptance of such Patent, Grant, or Commission, make and subscribe the aforesaid Declaration, or in Default thereof his Appointment to such Office, Employment or Place of Trust, and such Patent, Grant, or Commission, shall be wholly void.

VI. And be it further enacted, That the aforesaid Declaration shall be made and subscribed in His Majesty's High Court of Chancery, or in the Court of King's Bench, or at the Quarter Sessions of the County or Place where the Person so required to make the same shall reside; and the court in which such Declaration shall be so made and subscribed shall cause the same to be preserved among the Records of the said Court.

VII. Provided always, That no Naval Officer below the Rank of Rear Admiral, and no Military Officer below the rank of Major General in the Army or Colonel in the Militia, shall be required to make or subscribe the said Declaration, in respect of his Naval or Military Commission; and that no Commissioner of Customs, Excise, Stamps, or Taxes, or any Person holding any of the Offices concerned in the Collection, Management, or Receipt of the Revenues which are subject to the said Commissioners, or any of the Officers concerned in the Collection, Management, or Receipt of the Revenues subject to the Authority of the Postmaster General, shall be required to make or subscribe the said Declaration, in respect of their said Offices or Appointments: . . . [people returning from abroad required to make declaration within six months]. . . .

VIII. And be it further enacted, That all Persons now in the actual Possession of any Office, Command, Place, Trust, Service, or Employment, or in the Receipt of any Pay, Salary, Fee, or Wages, in respect of or as a Qualification for which, by virtue of or under any of the before-mentioned Acts or any other Act or Acts, they respectively ought to have heretofore taken or ought hereafter to receive the said Sacrament of the Lord's Supper, shall be and are hereby confirmed in the Possession and Enjoyment of their said several Offices, . . . [they are not subject to penalties regardless of failing to take the Sacrament] . . .; and that no Election of or Act done or to be done by any such Person or under his Authority, and not yet avoided, shall be hereafter questioned or avoided by reason of any such Omission or Neglect; . . .

IX. Provided nevertheless, That no Act done in the Execution of any of the Corporate or other Offices, Places, Trusts, or Commissions aforesaid, by any such Person omitting or neglecting as aforesaid, shall by reason thereof be void or voidable as to the Rights of any other Person not privy to such Omission or Neglect, or render such last-mentioned Person liable to any Action or Indictment.

31

ROMAN CATHOLIC EMANCIPATION ACT, 1829

Source: *Roman Catholic Emancipation Act*, 1829, 10 Geo. IV, c. 7

'Whereas by various Acts of Parliament certain Restraints and disabilities are imposed on the Roman Catholic Subjects of His Majesty, to which other Subjects of His Majesty are not liable: and Whereas it is expedient that such Restraints and Disabilities shall be from henceforth discontinued: and Whereas by various Acts certain Oaths and Declarations, commonly called the Declaration against Transubstantiation, and the Declaration against Transubstantiation and the Invocation of Saints and the Sacrifice of the Mass, as practised in the Church of *Rome*, are or may be required to be taken, made, and subscribed by the subjects of His Majesty, as Qualifications for sitting and voting in Parliament, and for the Enjoyment of certain Offices, Franchises, and Civil Rights:' Be it enacted . . . That from and after the Commencement of this Act all such Parts of the said Acts as require the said Declarations, . . . as a Qualification for sitting and voting in Parliament, or for the Exercise or Enjoyment of any Office, Franchise, or Civil Right, be and the same are (save as hereinafter provided and excepted) hereby repealed.

II. And be it enacted, That from and after the Commencement of this Act it shall be lawful for any Person professing the Roman Catholic Religion, being a Peer, or who shall after the Commencement of this Act be returned as a Member of the House of Commons, to sit and vote in either House of Parliament respectively, being in all other respects duly qualified to sit and vote therein, upon taking and subscribing the following Oath, instead of the Oaths of Allegiance, Supremacy, and Abjuration.

'I *A. B.* do sincerely promise and swear, That I will be faithful and bear true Allegiance to His Majesty King *George* the Fourth, and will defend him to the utmost of my Power against all Conspiracies and Attempts whatever, which shall be made against his Person, Crown, or Dignity; and I will do my utmost Endeavour to disclose and make known to His Majesty, his Heirs and Successors, all Treasons and traitorous Conspiracies which may be formed against Him or Them: and I do faithfully promise to maintain, support, and defend, to the utmost of my Power, the Succession of the Crown, which Succession, by an Act, intituled *An Act for the further Limitation of the Crown, and better securing the Rights and Liberties of the Subject*, is and stands limited to the Princess *Sophia*, Electress of *Hanover*, and the Heirs of her Body, being Protestants; hereby utterly renouncing and abjuring any Obedience or Allegiance unto any other Person claiming or pretending a Right to the Crown of this Realm: And I do further declare, That it is not an Article of my Faith, and that I do denounce, reject, and abjure the Opinion, that Princes excommunicated or deprived by the Pope, or any other Authority of the See of *Rome*, may be deposed or murdered by their Subjects, or by any Person whatsoever: And I do declare, That I do not believe that the Pope of *Rome*, or any other Foreign Prince, Prelate, Person, State, or Potentate, hath or ought to have any Temporal or Civil Jurisdiction, Power, Superiority, or Pre-eminence, directly or indirectly, within this Realm. I do swear, That I will defend to the utmost of my power the Settlement of Property within this Realm, as established by the Laws: And I do hereby disclaim, disavow, and solemnly abjure, any Intention to subvert the present Church Establishment, as settled by Law within this Realm: And I do solemnly swear, That I will never exercise any Privilege to which I am or may become entitled, to disturb or weaken the Protestant Religion, or Protestant Government in the United Kingdom: And I do solemnly, in the presence of God, profess, testify, and declare, That I do make this Declaration, and every Part thereof, in the plain and ordinary Sense of the Words of this Oath, without any Evasion, Equivocation, or mental Reservation whatever. So help me GOD.'

32

'NEWSPAPER STAMP DUTIES'

Edward Lytton Bulwer

Source: House of Commons, 21 August 1835

Mr. Edward Lytton Bulwer rose to submit a Motion to the House for the repeal of the Stamp-duties on Newspapers. The hon. Member said . . . The whole expression of public opinion, in a periodical shape, is at present confined to the narrowest oligarchy that ever disgraced a free country. No man can publish a newspaper – that is, no man can write periodically upon the news of the day, or the debates in Parliament, or any domestic or foreign affairs – without paying four-pence upon every sheet in the shape of a tax. The result is, that the legal market is altogether confined to great capitalists, and exclusive monopolists, while a large and cheap market is opened to smugglers. I am aware that if you take away the whole duty, papers such as the Times will still require an immense capital, but still a number of payers, upon a thousand subjects interesting to the great bulk of the population, will be published, which will not require so much capital. It is perfectly absurd to see only five or six morning papers for the active, thoughtful, and stirring population of this country. This is not the case in America, where a single district supports as many morning and evening papers as the whole of England. But I need only refer to England itself to show the operation of this tax. In 1792 there were thirteen morning and twenty evening papers published in London – although at that time the population numerically must have been much less, and the reading population not one half what it is at present. It is absurd to talk about the liberty of the Press in England so long as the taxes on knowledge continue as at present – it is in vain to make holyday speeches about it saying, "it is the very air we breathe, and if we have it not, we perish," when the Press is the only means of expressing the opinions of which the condition is a large capital and the result a severe monopoly. It has been urged that if the newspaper Press is rendered cheap, it will become bad and worthless, and that if the market is widened, the commodity will be deteriorated. Why, if this argument were used as to any other article of trade a man would be set down as an idiot. If a dozen persons only were allowed to sell spectacles, and a proposition was made to allow every person to sell them, would not the statesman who told you that in that case spectacles would be good for nothing, deserve to be laughed at? The analogy holds good with every thing – the greater the competition the greater the chance of excellence, and the wider the market, the better the commodity. But this truth obtains more with respect to literature than any thing else. Does the history of literature tell you that a man writes well in proportion as he is wealthy, and that the extent of his knowledge or genius is in proportion to his stock in the three per cents? I am afraid you will find that the reverse is the fact. If a tax of 200 per cent, which is that now imposed upon newspapers, were placed upon any other species of literature, it would long since have put an extinguisher upon all the best literature in the country. What extinguished the Spectator? – was it not the tax of one penny? – The eloquence of Addison and the wit of Steele, could not make head against a penny tax. How many Spectators in politics equally talented may you not have extinguished by a tax of four times the amount? I will ask my right hon. Friend what difference is there between political periodical writing and any other writing? Are they not subject to the same laws – created by the same intellect – influenced by the same competition, and improved by the same causes. There is only this difference between them, that political, and particularly periodical political writing, is much more generally useful and important than any other description. If I was a poor man, and that I had not read the Rambler, or the Spectator, or Shakespeare, or Milton, I do not well see how I should stand a greater chance of being imprisoned, or transported, or hanged. But were I a poor man and did not read the newspapers – if I did not know what new laws were passed surrounding me with punishments – if I did not know what was legal and what was illegal – I should be liable to suffer through ignorance, and thus tins tax of fourpence which keeps numbers of persons from obtaining the more useful knowledge, subjects them to crime, and exposes them to the gallows. I can compare the system to nothing but the monstrous tyranny of shutting men up in a dark room, and declaring that they shall be severely punished if they stumble against the numerous obstacles by which they are surrounded. I confess I do not share in the feelings entertained by some hon. Members against the present newspaper Press. Where a great power exists it is sometimes abused, but the wonder appears to me to be that its powers have been so seldom abused. I hope I have shown that I am above the meanness of flattering or fawning upon this formidable engine of praise or censure, by having been the first person to bring forward a substantive Motion for the Repeal of the existing monopoly; and, therefore, it is, that I think I may be allowed to bear witness to the talent, respectability, character, and accomplished education of the great mass of the gentlemen connected with the periodical Press. I use this, not as a compliment, but as an argument, in favour of my Motion. It is precisely because the Press is thus able and excellent that we ought to extend its advantages as widely as possible. Can any one suppose that these gentlemen will write worse when they have a larger community to address? But it is said, "if they write for the multitude they must pander to their base passions." Whoever makes that assertion knows very little about the multitude. Look at the papers which please the great mass of the people, and you will find articles on science, trade, education, the steam-engine, and matters which would appear tedious to us. They do not desire their bad passions to be aroused – they seek to have their minds enlightened. They live by labour and seek to know how that labour may be best directed. I am afraid it is we – the idle rich – "the lords of luxury and ease," who require a false and meretricious excitement – who alone support the disgraces of the Press – who encourage the slander and scandal, the venom and frivolity, which were first wrought into sundry libels, not by a radical journal, not by a heartless demagogue print, but by a paper professing a hatred of democratic principles and dignifying by its support the Tory cause. It pretends to furnish the gossip of the Court, and the tittle tattle of the aristocracy. If you look at the large Newspapers which circulate among the great mass of the people, you will find in them the most varied information, the most argumentative writing, and a great freedom from private calumny, vulgar slander, and personal abuse. But it may be said – If you make the Press free, many dangerous and revolutionary political doctrines may be published. Doubtless, there will be, as now, doctrines of all sorts – the good and the bad? But who is to decide what is good and what bad? Some hon. Members on the other side of the House tell us that the doctrines of the present Government are revolutionary and dangerous; whereas, from what I have heard this very night, if I were asked what doctrines were most likely to weaken the just influence of the Crown, separate the different classes, incense the people, and produce and hasten the course of revolution? – I should say that it was the doctrine of the Conservatives. Who then shall decide the question as to what is good and what is bad – what is useful, and what is revolutionary? None can do so: scarcely time itself can decide it. In the words of an able writer – "Truth requires no inscription to distinguish it from darkness; and all that Truth wants is the liberty of expression." Has not the terror of the propagation of dangerous doctrines been used against the progress of enlightenment? Is it not for this that censors have been placed upon books, and inquisitors upon opinions? What effect have these prosecutions produced? The French Court prohibited the works of Voltaire, and Voltaire became at once endowed with the power to shake old opinion to its centre. Geneva burnt the Social Contract of Rousseau, and out of its ashes arose the phoenix of its influence. Tom Paine had not sold ten copies of his notorious work, when the English Government thought fit to prosecute him, and within a week from that period there were sold 30,000 copies. Government never has prevented, and never can prevent, the propagation of dangerous doctrines by prohibitions, either in the shape of a tax or a law – the only effect of persecution is to render the doctrines more dangerous and the people more eager to learn it. If I want a new proof of the truth of this argument, do I not find it in the very tax I ask you to repeal? For how many years have you been endeavouring to put down the unstamped Press, whose doctrines are alleged to be dangerous, and for how many years has it enjoyed impunity, and deluged every manufacturing town? The market has been literally overstocked with its productions. If you were to repeal the whole tax to-morrow, there would not be a single new publication of these dangerous inflammatory doctrines, for during the last seven or eight years every one who wished to publish them has done so with impunity. By the imposition of the tax upon the more respectable class, you have prevented any reply to these dangerous publications. You have given up the field to those who have sown it with noxious weeds, and prevented the good husbandman from labouring in it. You are now at last embarked in an obstinate war with the unstamped Press – a war in which I am sure you will not succeed. I ask the right hon. Gentleman, does he think for a moment that he can succeed so long as the tax is 200 per cent upon the article smuggled? My right hon. Friend is aware, better than myself, that the only way to diminish smuggling, where it has risen to an enormous height, is to reduce the tax, and that is what I now urge upon my right hon. Friend. I do not ask a total repeal, but only a reduction to one penny. By this reduction, I think, a very great advantage will be gained. We shall materially extend the advantages of knowledge, without in the least diminishing the amount of revenue. The Stamp duty at present produces (after allowing for the discount) three pence and a fraction upon each paper; and if it were reduced to one penny, we should require only three times the present number of papers to be sold to replace the loss suffered by the revenue. Does not every man acquainted with the habits of the working classes know – does not every man who is aware of their extraordinary desire for knowledge, scientific and political, feel that we should then have three times as many papers published as at present? Besides, my right hon. Friend having made this concession, would then be justified in coming down to this House, and demanding new and more efficient laws for the suppression of smuggling – the result of which would hring all, or nearly all the slippery fish that at present creep out of the meshes, into my right hon. Friend's net. In addition to the increased circulation, there would be the increased advertisement duty, and the increased paper duty; so that without being at all sanguine, I say that the revenue would not, by any means, be a loser. Suppose the Stamp Duty reduced, as I have proposed, to one penny, such papers as the Times and Chronicle and the Herald, which require a large capital, would not be able to sell for less than fourpence. But new papers not requiring so large a capital would be called into existence – papers partly literary, and containing the news of the day – half scientific and half commercial, which would thus attract many readers. Above all, many religious publications would be called into existence, supported by different religious societies, and coming forth two or three times a week. Thus a new class of periodicals would be called into existence, and all productive to the revenue in three ways – by the Stamp Duty, the Advertisement Duty, and the Paper Duty. It was stated in a periodical, a short time since, that if the whole duty were taken off, ten times as many papers would be published as at present; and, therefore, with only a tax of a penny, I have a right to assume that three times as many would be published. The amount of a penny tax upon three times the present number of sheets, would be 400,000l. I greatly underrate the Paper Duty if I take the increase at 30,000l., and the increased Advertisement Duty at 20,000l., making a total of 450,000l., which equals the sum produced by the present fourpenny tax. The increased Paper Duty I have greatly underrated, as a high duty diminishes the profit and the sale to a very considerable extent. In a calculation made respecting the Penny Magazine, it has been shown that if a tax of one penny was imposed, the sale would be decreased one-tenth, and comparing the increased duty on the stamp with the loss of revenue on the paper, it has been clearly ascertained that the Exchequer would lose, on that paper alone, 400l. a-year. Apply this argument generally, and you will see how much the revenue loses by the present high rate of duty. The system has robbed the revenue on the one hand of more than it has paid into it on the other. I shall not detain the House much longer; but, before I conclude, I must say, that the present Government owes something to the provincial Press; and, with few exceptions, the Provincial Press has petitioned for some relief. The provincial Press has supported the Government nobly, and without its assistance I doubt much if any liberal Government could have made head against the determined and vehement attacks of three morning papers of great circulation and influence. Yet the provincial papers are cramped in their exertions, and limited in their power, by the audience they address being narrowed and limited by the Stamp Duty. You owe something also to those who, adopting opinions more (I should say) determined and dreaded than your own, have yet supported you frankly and generously. The panegyric which my right hon. Friend has to-night pronounced upon that class who, professing these opinions have yet compromised them to a certain extent, and given to the Government the independent and undivided support, is another argument in favour of my Motion; for there is no concession which will be looked upon as a gracier on, nor none which will be repaid more largely and generously by the party who, whether in praise or blame, are called the Radical party, than a concession upon this point. If any body of men have ever acted from the purest public motives, patriotically and disinterestedly, I believe it is that party, and, therefore, I do say that my right hon. Friend owes them some concession. The last argument I shall use is, that the Government owe it to themselves and to their own consistency, to make some concession to the Press. They will not in such a case be sacrificing their own opinions to please a great body of the public, and of their supporters – they will be merely following up those sentiments which they have expressed on former occasions. There are few now on the Treasury Bench who have not, on some former occasion, expressed themselves favourable to the measure. The right hon. the President of the Board of Trade, the noble Lord, the Secretary for Ireland, the right hon. the Chancellor of the Exchequer, and even his Majesty's present Attorney-General have given dignity to the question by their acknowledged affection to its principle. I have the greatest confidence, therefore, in the present Government, and I hope upon this question, as upon all others, I shall live to see them faithful to the great principle of Reform, which proportions power to intelligence, and which, while it renders the Constitution more popular prevents the danger by rendering the people more enlightened. So strong is my reliance upon the objects and intentions of the present Government, that I am satisfied the more widely their sentiments are diffused and known, the more generally will they be approved. I regret to see them shut themselves out from half the national enthusiasm, and half tbe popular support which would be theirs, were the laws they enact, and the principles they advocate, brought cheaply, easily, and familiarly before that great class of the community for whose benefit they have laboured, and in whose cause they have won their most imperishable renown. It is with this hope that I now move that the House do resolve itself into a Committee of the whole House, to consider the question that, for the more general diffusion of knowledge, it is expedient that the Stamp Duty on Newspapers be reduced to one penny.

33

'PUBLIC MEETINGS IN THE METROPOLIS'

Charles Bradlaugh

Source: House of Commons, 1 March 1888

MR. BRADLAUGH (Northampton), who had given notice of the following, as an Amendment to Sir Charles Russell's Motion, at end, add – And that, in the opinion of this House, it would ensure much greater confidence in the administration of the Law if a full and public inquiry were granted into the alleged unlawful assembly in Trafalgar Square on Sunday, November 13, 1887, and the conduct of the Police in connection therewith, said, without discourtesy he would not enter into the full discussion of the speech of the hon. Gentleman the Member for Westminster (Mr. Burdett-Coutts). The hon. Gentleman quoted as an enactment that which was not one. The hon. Member had told the House that it had been enacted by 57 Geo. III., c. 29, that no meeting whatever could take place within a mile of Westminster when Parliament or the Law Courts were sitting. That was simply not a fact. It was perfectly true that some meetings must not take place. These meetings were specified, and it was in kindness to the hon. Member that he asked him to complete the quotation in order to save him from making a blunder. He would not reply further to the speech of the hon. Gentleman. [Cries of "Read."] It was not absolutely necessary that legislators should know Statutes; but they had scarcely a right to oblige a Member at that hour of the night (11.20) to read a Statute to which he had referred specifically, and ignorance did not justify interruption.

MR. BURDETT-COUTTS said, that he preferred very much to be thoroughly sat upon, and as he had been challenged to read the quotation he should now very much like to hear the hon. Gentleman read it himself.

MR. BRADLAUGH said, he fancied that the operation to which the hon. Gentleman had referred had already been performed, and perhaps the hon. Member would now allow him to proceed. He wished to address himself to the speech of the right hon. Gentleman the Secretary of State for the Home Department (Mr. Matthews), and he did so with some misgivings, because none could deny the eloquence which the right hon. Gentleman brought to bear upon the subject. He regretted that it was the eloquence of the Advocate rather than of a Member of the Executive intrusted almost with judicial duty. The right hon. Gentleman left a number of important points put to him by the hon. and learned Gentleman the Member for South Hackney (Sir Charles Russell) without reply. The right hon. Gentleman made no answer in commenting on a letter sent from the Chief Commissioner of Police to the manager of Mrs. Weldon's meeting, although on the face of it it distinctly recognized the right which he denied. The right hon. Gentleman made no answer to the habitual user of the Square for more than 30 years as a right except to say that it was by licence and permission, when the facts quoted were facts of distinct disproof of any such licence or permission, and of distinct assertion of the user of right. The right hon. Gentleman took no notice of the appeal made by the hon. and learned Member for South Hackney as to the advice given by the Law Officers of the Crown, which was quoted by Sir George Grey in that House, and which was in the Home Office for reference. The right hon. Gentleman did not venture to suggest that there was any mis-statement, but he left Sir George Grey's declaration that he had been advised that the public had a right of meeting in Trafalgar Square entirely untouched. Sir George Grey, on the 24th July, 1886, said that when the meeting was about to be held in Trafalgar Square he stated, as far as he was informed, that it was a legal meeting; that any meeting at which language was held that was calculated to produce a breach of the peace was illegal, but that a meeting held to discuss Parliamentary reform was not in itself illegal; that he gave directions to the police in regard to that meeting; and that he begged to inform an hon. Member who asked what means he had taken to preserve the peace that he gave directions to the Commissioner of Police that he was not to interfere with the meeting as long as it was legally and peacefully held. The right hon. Gentleman the Home Secretary, again, had entirely avoided the challenge put to him by the hon. and learned Member for South Hackney as to why he did not allow the case of Mr. W. Saunders to be tried. He would suggest to the right hon. Gentleman why he did not. He would suggest that the Law Officers of the Crown pointed out that, although Mr. Saunders had disobeyed the proclamation and held his meeting in spite of the right hon. Gentleman, it was not an unlawful meeting, and that the question which would have to be tried would be whether it was unlawful from being held in Trafalgar Square, and that the right hon. Gentleman was advised that he would be beaten on that issue, and, therefore, he abandoned the prosecution. The matter which had to be considered on his Amendment differed very considerably from the question raised by the hon. and learned Member for South Hackney; although his Amendment was in no sense hostile to the hon. and learned Member's Motion, but only an addition to it. There were two questions before the House for the expression of its opinion upon them. One of those questions was whether there was a right of public open meeting in England. He said, clearly, that there was. Was there such a right in the Metropolis? Notwithstanding what the hon. and learned Attorney General for the Duchy of Cornwall (Mr. C. Hall) said, he contended that there was. Was there such a right of meeting in Trafalgar Square? Notwithstanding the declaration, unqualified and unmeasured, of the right hon. Gentleman the Home Secretary, he equally contended that there was. But if there were not it would be a sad thing for this country. The only phrase, which lingered in his memory, of the speech of the hon. Member who had just sat down, was that free speech was of no English Party. That was true. It was only 160 years ago that the Conservatives – the Tories as they then called themselves – were pleading for what he should plead that night. It was because at that time they were denied the liberty of public meeting and were harassed when they tried to exercise their right, that they pleaded before the mother of Parliaments for affirmation for them of that of which they would to-day deny the use to the people. He asked hon. Members differing from him in politics to reflect on the great difficulties they put in the way of men who might hold strong views, but who desired to guide their fellow-countrymen wisely and peacefully in seeking useful reforms, if they took away from the people of England the only outlet and safety-valve which the poor had for making known their grievances to the world. The hon. and learned Member for South Hackney had dwelt on the great value of the right of public meeting. Now, he did not pretend that that right had always been wisely used by himself, but he did pretend that he had done his best his whole life through to keep it peacefully, orderly, and law-abiding. When he had thought that right unfairly challenged he had insisted upon it against the Government itself. The right hon. Gentleman the Home Secretary was good enough to congratulate him that he had been successful. But if the right hon. Gentleman had proved that he had been successful in over-riding the law that would not have been a matter for congratulation across the floor of the House. It was matter of congratulation, because he had kept to the legal right and he had been content always to argue the questions raised step by step before the tribunals of the country, which he found did justice without reference to who was the man that was pleading before them; and he said that equally when he was defeated and when he was successful. Well, because some men might use violent language, was that a good reason why the whole right of public meetings should be withheld and denied? If that was attempted they might provoke an uprising which would require far stronger brains and stouter hearts to meet it than were possessed by the present occupants of the Treasury Bench. He interrupted the right hon. Gentleman in order to ask him for the names of the speakers whom he quoted. He was sorry to say with the exception of one name the right hon. Gentleman did not give them, because he alleged that one particular speaker, who urged the setting fire to London in several places, was the speaker whose speech gave the Government the right to interfere with this meeting. He told the right hon. Gentleman his excuse for his interruption, that if he could identify the name he was prepared with evidence to show that the speaker who used that language had been seen in company with the police, but not in custody. The right hon. Gentleman, with a skill of tongue which he did not possess, said that he did not know that the police were not fit company; but surely the right hon. Gentleman hardly misunderstood his suggestion. What he was prepared to do if the name be given – it was difficult to make a charge upon it until he knew the name – was to show that the man who was in custody in connexion with the Trafalgar Square meetings was dismissed by the magistrate, and that, while in custody, he pointed out from a window overlooking the yard to Mr. Burleigh – a reporter of the Press – a man in plain clothes with the police in the yard, who, he said, was the man who used those words in the Square. The communication he had received might be untrue; but the writer stated that he was prepared to make the statement in a formal way so as to subject him to prosecution for giving false evidence. While not committing himself on the subject he was ready to hand the letter over in order that an investigation might be made, provided he was first furnished with the name of the person who was supposed to have made the speech. As to the right of meeting, he pointed out that the late Lord Derby, speaking in the House of Lords on July 24, 1866, said: – "There is no desire on the part of anyone to interfere with that which is the right of British subjects – namely, to assemble for the discussion of political and public questions wherever they do not infringe upon public or private rights." – (3 Hansard, [184] 1372.) But there was such a desire manifested that evening. The Government, as he understood, claimed for the Executive the right to guess when a meeting ought to be stopped. [Mr. MATTHEWS dissented.] The right hon. Gentleman claimed for the Executive that whenever they had reason to think that a meeting would be unlawful they might stop it. The Executive should have no such right. If they had such a right Parliament should take it away, because it placed all meetings at the mercy of the Executive. The Executive ought to have a right to interfere if the avowed object was unlawful, or at the moment when the breaking of the peace had begun at the meeting. The Executive ought to have the right to arrest any persons guilty of seditious speaking at the meeting; but the Executive had no right whatever to imagine that any public meeting, however numerous, would be unlawful, and, therefore, to prevent it; still less had it the right to fasten upon one meeting the sins of another, or upon one set of men the sins of another set. It was a matter of common knowledge in Europe now that one Government, at any rate, had not hesitated to employ agents provocateurs in Geneva in order to utilize them against the men whom they were endeavouring to punish in Berlin. Although he was quite sure that it would be too dangerous an experiment for any Government to get found out at in this country today, he could not forget that our Parliamentary record showed that within the space of 60 years such dangerous and wicked experiments had been made and had been exposed by Committees of the House. In the charge of Baron Alderson in the case of Vincent, quoted by the hon. and learned Gentleman the Member for South Hackney, it was stated as distinctly as words could be that – There is no doubt that the people of this country have a perfect right to meet for the purpose of stating what are or even what they consider to be their grievances. That right they always have had, and I trust always will have. It was because he (Mr. Bradlaugh) adhered to that view that he intended to charge upon the Government that night the mischief which arose out of the Trafalgar Square meetings. The Government first vacillated, forbade and then permitted, changed its mind and purpose, now threatened and now did not, took notes of treasonable and seditious language, now prosecuted those who were misleading the people, and then punished the people who had no part in the utterances. The right hon. Gentleman the Home Secretary had been good enough to give the House the limits of the right of public meeting, saying that meetings must be held for a lawful purpose in a place where the public have a right to meet. And then the right hon. Gentleman built on that definition the conclusion that Trafalgar Square was not a place where the public had such a right. He (Mr. Bradlaugh) believed that Trafalgar Square was a thoroughfare and something more. It was also a place of public resort. It was not a thoroughfare for traffic over which carts and carriages might go; but it was like Hampstead Heath and Primrose Hill, a place where people might resort to amuse themselves or in the exercise of their political rights. For the last 50 or 60 years progress without violence or collision had been possible in this country, because successive Governments, except, unfortunately, in Ireland, had allowed all sections of the community to express their opinions, however strong, with the greatest possible freedom. The agitation for the Charter, which might have been revolutionary, was thus a movement of reform, and the bulk of the points of the Charter were now the law of the land. There was scarcely any great reform which had not been achieved by the outside pressure of the people, and there had been many great crises in our history where the voice of the people had gone for truth, for peace, and for progress, when the Government of the moment was for war, for hindrance, and for retrogression. In the Metropolis they had a population larger than that of Scotland, and where were their buildings in which they could meet? They were too few and too costly. But for a mere accident in his own case it would not be possible to get a hall in the Metropolis. On one occasion he was in St. James's Hall when the gas went out, and he managed to keep the audience quiet; since then he had been very much favoured by the proprietors. But St. James's Hall would not hold more than 5,000 people. There was a population of over 4,000,000, and there ought to be some place where the people could assemble in the exercise of their political rights. Mere numbers should not carry terror; they did not create terror when they wanted them to welcome Royalty in different parts of the town. He had been present at 40 or 50 meetings in Trafalgar Square, and he admitted the great responsibility of those who called them there. It was a right which should not be lightly used. He was quite ready to admit that the Government should regulate those meetings, and the Government, ever since the Parks' Regulation Act of 1872, had the power to lay down regulations for them, but had never done so. The meeting in question was convened by the Federation of the London Clubs. He was sorry not to see the right hon. Gentleman the Chancellor of the Exchequer (Mr. Goschen) in his place, because the right hon. Gentleman had in the Provinces spoken of those clubs with great contempt, saying that they were in debt. The London Working Men's Clubs concerned were not rich, but they were not so much in debt as some clubs – which could be named – were. It was a libel to say that these clubs were only houses in which five or six men could live. The right hon. Gentleman spoke also of them as places where a few men met to drink. The right hon. Gentleman the Chancellor of the Exchequer libelled these London Working Men's Clubs. Last night he (Mr. Bradlaugh) attended one club with 1,800 members, with lecture hall which would hold some 500, with library and reading room, and this not the largest club even in that district. The members of these clubs had rough hands, but they were men who worked to live. He knew those working men, he was born amongst them, he belonged to them; and, so far as he could, he would defend their rights. The meeting of November 13 was called by the Federation of London Clubs, which were not the drinking houses the right hon. Gentleman the Chancellor of the Exchequer represented them, but embraced some 30,000 or 40,000 men. At his own meetings in Trafalgar Square he had had 2,500 stewards chosen from these clubs, and that was the way in which he had been prepared to resist illegal force if used against him. He admitted that if the police were on the spot first the people had no right to break in; he had never encouraged people to break the law, but to stand by their rights. With regard to the Acts of Parliament relating to Trafalgar Square, the quotations from and references to these by the hon. and learned Member for South Hackney has been entirely ignored and evaded by the Home Secretary, who repeated the fallacy that the bulk of the Square had been formed from the private property of the Monarch. This was not so. There were plans specifically referred to in the Statutes, and these plans showed that the bulk of the land had been private property, and that the King's Mews only formed a very small portion of the land. That private property had been bought by public money in order that there might be an open space, which the right hon. Gentleman now wished to close by his mere will. He (Mr. Bradlaugh) was sorry that the right hon. Gentleman had thought it right to introduce the name of the Sovereign and to speak of the Sovereign as the private owner of the land. The Sovereign of this country had no rights, except by the law, and the user of Trafalgar Square was not in the Sovereign to hold or to withhold. The Home Secretary is reported in The Times of December 12th to have stated to a deputation which waited on him at the Home Office, that "The public have no right of meeting in Trafalgar Square. It is only by sufferance and permission of the Queen they do meet there." And to-night he has talked of Her Majesty as the private owner on whose sufferance only the public might use the Square. At Bow Street Mr. Poland held the same monstrous doctrine, and contended in Mr. Saunders' case (The Times, November 18th) that "no person had any right to make speeches in Trafalgar Square," "it was the property of the Crown," and that the proclamation of Sir Charles Warren was "under no Statute, but under the Common Law, and as an officer of the Crown." The Crown had no right to interfere with public meetings in this country, except where Statute gave it to the Executive representing it. Personally, the Sovereign had no other right than the law defined. The Sovereign was the chief magistrate and first servant of the State, but the law was master alike over the Sovereign and the meanest of her subjects. The right hon. Gentleman had attached importance to the 3rd Section of the Act, which incorporated the Metropolitan Police Act. But the Metropolitan Police Act gave no power to the Commissioner of Police to prevent meetings in Trafalgar Square. All it did was, by Section 52, to make it lawful for the Commissioner of Police from time to time, and as occasion should require, to make regulations for the route to be observed by all carts, carriages, horses, and persons, and to prevent obstruction in the streets and thoroughfares, and in all times of public processions, rejoicings, or illuminations, to give to the constables instructions to prevent disorder and to prevent obstruction of the thoroughfares in the neighbourhood of Parliament, the public offices, courts of law, theatres, and other places of public resort, and in any case where the streets might be thronged or liable to obstruction. ["Hear, hear!"] Yes; regulating it, but not forbidding it, and the best proof of that was contained in the 9th rule in the next Section. When there was any great procession, the Chief Commissioner of Police had imposed upon him the duty of making such provision as would render as little as possible the necessary obstruction consistent with the happening of that event. He contended that there was nothing in the decisions which had been pronounced which gave any sort of credence to the claim made by this Officer of the Crown to prevent meetings. It was impossible for any great theatrical performance to be held without causing some obstruction; but the Chief Commissioner had no right to prevent the performance taking place, or to bludgeon the people. The Commissioner was only to do his best to make the obstruction cause as little injury as possible to the people. At that hour (two minutes to 12 o'clock) he thought that he would not be consulting the convenience of the House in entering upon another division of his speech; and he, therefore, begged to move the adjournment of the debate.

34

(INDUSTRIAL ACTION) TAFF VALE CASE, DECISION OF MR. JUSTICE FAREWELL

Source: (Industrial Action) Taff Vale Case, Decision of Mr. Justice Farewell, 1901

The defendant society have taken out a summons to strike out their name as defendants, on the ground that they are neither a corporation nor an individual and cannot be sued in a quasi-corporate or any other capacity. Failing this, they contend that no injunction ought to be granted against them. I reserved judgment last week on these two points, because the first is of very great importance, and counsel were unable to assist me by citing any reported case in which the question had been argued and decided.

Now it is undoubtedly true that a trade union is neither a corporation nor an individual, nor a partnership between a number of individuals; but this does not by any means conclude the case. A trade union, as defined by s. 16 of the Trade Union Act, 1876, "means any combination, whether temporary or permanent, for regulating the relations between workmen and masters, or between workmen and workmen, or between masters and masters, or for imposing restrictive conditions on the conduct of any trade or business, whether such combination would or would not, if the principal Act had not been passed, have been deemed to have been an unlawful combination by reason of some one or more of its purposes being in restraint of trade". It is an association of men which almost invariably owes its legal validity to the Trade Union Acts, 1871 and 1876. In the present case the foundation of the argument that I have heard on behalf of the society is that it is an illegal association – an argument that would have more weight if the action related to the enforcement of any contract, and were not an action in tort. The questions I have to consider are what, according to the true construction of the Trade Union Acts, has the legislature enabled the trade unions to do, and what, if any, liability does a trade union incur for wrongs done to others in the exercise of its authorised powers? The Acts commence by legalising the usual trade union contracts, and proceed to establish a registry of trade unions, to give to each trade union an exclusive right to the name in which it is registered, authorise it, through the medium of trustees to own a limited amount of real estate, and unlimited personal estate "for the use and benefit of such trade union and the members thereof"; provide that it shall have officers and treasurers, and render them liable to account; requires that annual returns be made to the registry of the assets and liabilities and receipts and expenditure of the society; imposing a penalty on the trade union for non-compliance; and permit it to amalgamate with other trade unions and to be wound up. The funds of the society are appropriated to the purposes of the society, and their misappropriation can be restrained by injunction . . . and on a winding up, such funds are distributed among the members in accordance with the rules of the society. . . . Further, the Act of 1871 contains a schedule of matters which must be provided for in the rules. The object and the limitations of the Acts are stated by Sir George Jessel in Rigby v. Connell ((1880), 14 Ch. D. 489) as follows: "That Act was passed, no doubt, primarily with a view to preventing the treasurers and secretaries and officers of these societies from robbing them; that was the chief object. It was discovered that some of these men, abusing the confidence reposed in them, took advantage of the law which made these societies illegal, by appropriating their funds and property to their own use. That, no doubt, was one of the principal objects, and therefore the Act was passed to get at these men. Another object was this: there was a great difficulty in suing and getting their property from third persons, and one object of the Act was to enable these societies to sue in respect of their property, and also to enable them to hold property such as a house or an office, but it was not intended that the contracts entered into by the members of the society should be made legal contracts *inter se*, so that courts of justice should interfere to enforce them. If that had been intended the result would have been this, that an agreement between a number of workmen once entered into, compelling them to work in a particular manner, or to abstain from working in a particular manner, would have been enforceable according to law, and to a certain extent would have reduced some portion of the workmen to a condition of something like serfdom and slavery. Of course the legislature, by interfering, had no idea of doing anything of that sort." But these limitations merely restrict the actual enforcement of trade union contracts by action or suit, and do not affect the status of the association to which such members belong. Now, although a corporation and an individual or individuals may be the only entity known to the common law who can sue or be sued, it is competent to the legislature to give to an association of individuals which is neither a corporation nor a partnership, nor an individual, a capacity for owning property and acting by agents, and such capacity in the absence of express enactment to the contrary involves the necessary correlative of liability to the extent of such property for the acts and defaults of such agents. It is beside the mark to say of such an association that it is unknown to the common law. The legislature has legalised it, and it must be dealt with by the courts according to the intention of the legislature. For instance, a lease in perpetuity is unknown at common law, but such a lease granted by one railway company to another when confirmed by the legislature becomes valid and binding (*see* Sir George Jessel's judgment in Sevenoaks etc. Ry. Co. v. London, Chatham and Dover Ry. Co. (1879), 11 Ch. D. 625, 635); nor can it be said for this purpose that the association is illegal, for the legislature by ss 2 and 3 of the Act of 1871 has rendered legal the usual purposes of a trade union, and has further enabled the trade union to carry into effect those purposes by the provision to which I have already referred. This is not a case of suing in contract, to which the provisions of s. 4 of the Act would apply; it is an action in tort, and the real question is whether on the true construction of the Trade Union Acts the legislature has legalised an association which can own property and can act by agents by intervening in labour disputes between employers and employed, but which cannot be sued in respect of such acts.

Now the legislature in giving a trade union the capacity to own property and the capacity to act by agents has, without incorporating it, given it two of the essential qualities of a corporation – essential, I mean, in respect of the liability for tort, for a corporation can only act by its agents, and can only be made to pay by means of its property. The principle on which corporations have been held liable in respect of wrongs committed by its servants or agents in the course of their service and for the benefit of the employer – *qui sentit commodum sentire debet et onus* – (*see* Mersey Docks Trustees v. Gibbs (1866), L.R. 1, H.L. 93) is as applicable to the case of a trade union as to that of a corporation. If the contention of the defendant society were well-founded, the legislature has authorised the creation of numerous bodies of men capable of owning great wealth and of acting by agents with absolutely no responsibility for the wrongs that they may do to other persons by the use of that wealth and the employment of those agents. They would be at liberty (I do not at all suggest that the defendant society would so act) to disseminate libels broadcast, or to hire men to reproduce the rattening methods that disgraced Sheffield thirty or forty years ago, and their victims would have nothing to look to for damages but the pockets of the individuals, usually men of small means, who acted as their agents. That this is a consideration that may fairly be taken into account appears from the opinion of the judges given to the House of Lords in the Mersey Docks Case (L.R. 1, H.L. 120): "We cannot think that it was the intention of the legislature to deprive a shipowner who pays dues to a wealthy trading company, such as the St Catherine's Dock Company, for instance, of all recourse against it, and to substitute the personal responsibility of a harbour master, no doubt a respectable person in his way, but whose whole means, generally speaking, would not be equal to more than a very small percentage of the damages, when there are any." The proper rule of construction of statutes such as these is that in the absence of express contrary intention, the legislature intends that the creature of the statute shall have the same duties, and that its funds shall be subject to the same liabilities as the general law would impose on a private individual doing the same thing. It would require very clear and express words of enactment to induce me to hold that the legislature had in fact legalised the existence of such irresponsible bodies with such wide responsibility for evil. Not only is there nothing in the Acts to lead me to such a conclusion, but ss 15 and 16 of the Act of 1876 point to a contrary conclusion; nor do I see any reason for saying that the society cannot be sued in tort in their registered name. Sects 8 and 9 of the Act of 1871 expressly provide for actions in respect of property being brought by and against the trustees, and this express intention impliedly excludes such trustees from being sued in tort. If, therefore, I am right in concluding that the society are liable in tort, the action must be against them in their registered name. The acts complained of are the acts of the association. They are acts done by their agents in the course of the management and direction of a strike; the undertaking such management and direction is one of the main objects of the defendant society, and is perfectly lawful; but the society, in undertaking such management and direction, undertook also the responsibility for the manner in which the strike is carried out. The fact that no action could be brought at law or in equity to compel the society to interfere or refrain from interfering in the strike is immaterial; it is not a question of the rights of members of the society, but of the wrong done to persons outside the society. For such wrongs, arising as they do from the wrongful conduct of the agents of the society in the course of managing a strike which is a lawful object of the society, the defendant society is, in my opinion, liable.

I have come to this conclusion on principle, and on the construction of the Acts, and there is nothing to the contrary in any of the cases cited by the defendants' counsel. . . .

35

ALIENS ACT, 1905

Source: *Aliens Act*, 1905, 5 Ed. 7, c. 13

An immigrant shall not be landed in the United Kingdom from an immigrant ship except at a port at which there is an immigration officer appointed under this Act, and shall not be landed at any such port without the leave of that officer given after an inspection of the immigrants made by him on the ship, or elsewhere if the immigrants are conditionally disembarked for the purpose, in company with a medical inspector, such inspection to be made as soon as practicable, and the immigration officer shall withhold leave in the case of any immigrant who appears to him to be an undesirable immigrant within the meaning of this section.

| Power to prevent the landing of undesirable immigrants. |

...

(3) For the purposes of this section an immigrant shall be considered an undesirable immigrant –

(*a*) if he cannot show that he has in his possession or is in a position to obtain the means of decently supporting himself and his dependents (if any); or
(*b*) if he is a lunatic or an idiot, or owing to any disease or infirmity appears likely to become a charge upon the rates or otherwise a detriment to the public; or
(*c*) if he has been sentenced in a foreign country with which there is an extradition treaty for a crime, not being an offence of a political character, which is, as respects that country, an extradition crime within the meaning of the Extradition Act, 1870; or
(*d*) if an expulsion order under this Act has been made in his case;

| 33 & 34 Vict. c. 52. |

but, in the case of an immigrant who proves that he is seeking admission to this country solely to avoid prosecution or punishment on religious or political grounds or for an offence of a political character, or persecution, involving danger of imprisonment or danger to life or limb, on account of religious belief, leave to land shall not be refused on the ground merely of want of means, or the probability of his becoming a charge on the rates, nor shall leave to land be withheld in the case of an immigrant who shows to the satisfaction of the immigration officer or board concerned with the case that, having taken his ticket in the United Kingdom and embarked direct therefrom for some other country immediately after a period of residence in the United Kingdom of not less than six months, he has been refused admission in that country and returned direct therefrom to a port in the United Kingdom, and leave to land shall not be refused merely on the ground of want of means to any immigrant who satisfies the immigration officer or board concerned with the case that he was born in the United Kingdom, his father being a British subject.

...

EXPULSION OF UNDESIRABLE ALIENS

3. – (1) The Secretary of State may, if he thinks fit, make an order (in this Act referred to as an expulsion order) requiring an alien to leave the United Kingdom within a time fixed by the order, and thereafter to remain out of the United Kingdom –

	Power of Secretary of State to make an expulsion order.

(a) if it is certified to him by any court (including a court of summary jurisdiction) that the alien has been convicted by that court of any felony, or misdemeanour, or other offence for which the court has power to impose imprisonment without the option of a fine, or of an offence under paragraph twenty-two or twenty-three of section three hundred and eighty-one of the Burgh Police (Scotland) Act, 1892, or of an offence as a prostitute under section seventy-two of the Towns Improvement (Ireland) Act, 1854, or paragraph eleven of section fifty-four of the Metropolitan Police Act, 1839, and that the court recommend that an expulsion order should be made in his case, either in addition to or in lieu of his sentence; and

55 & 56 Vict. c. 55.
2 & 3 Vict. c. 47.
17 & 18 Vict. c. 103.

(b) if it is certified to him by a court of summary jurisdiction after proceedings taken for the purpose within twelve months after the alien has last entered the United Kingdom, in accordance with rules of court made under section twenty-nine of the Summary Jurisdiction Act, 1879, that the alien –

42 & 43 Vict. c. 49.

   (i) has within three months from the time at which proceedings for the certificate are commenced been in receipt of any such parochial relief as disqualifies a person for the parliamentary franchise, or been found wandering without ostensible means of subsistence, or been living under insanitary conditions due to overcrowding; or

(ii) has entered the United Kingdom after the passing of this Act, and has been sentenced in a foreign country with which there is an extradition treaty for a crime not being an offence of a political character which is as respects that country an extradition crime within the meaning of the Extradition Act, 1870.

(2) If any alien in whose case an expulsion order has been made is at any time found within the United Kingdom in contravention of the order, he shall be guilty of an offence under this Act.

36

'TRADE DISPUTES BILL'

Lord Loreburn

Source: House of Lords, 4 December 1906

This Bill is substantially the same as that which was introduced in the House of Commons in the year 1903. I was a supporter of it then, and I had some share in drawing the Bill for those friends of mine who were on the Trade Union Council. In 1903 it was defeated in a Conservative House of Commons by thirty votes. It was brought in again in 1904, and was carried by twenty-nine votes. In 1905 further argument was held in the House, the Bill was more fully understood and more discussed, and in a Conservative House of Commons it was carried by a majority of 122.

Then came the general election, and the Bill of the Trade Union Congress in 1906 was carried by a majority of 350. The Government Bill passed the Second Reading without a division at all. But that did not conclude the interesting part of the career of this Bill, for I am practically right in saying that no employer of labour in the House of Commons had a word to say against it; and when the Bill came to a Third Reading Mr. Balfour recommended his Party not to divide against it, and therefore it conies up to your Lordships sealed with the unanimous approval, so far as divisions go, both on the Second Reading and the Third Reading, of the House of Commons. I respectfully commend to your Lordships' attention those facts as being full of significance, for I am not one of those who believe that our countrymen are so wanting in moral courage as to be afraid of opposing a bad Bill for electoral reasons. It was because the Bill could be justified by argument, as I am about to endeavour to justify it here, that the House of Commons came to the conclusion at which they arrived.

There was a Royal Commission preceding this Bill. It was constituted by the late Government. It consisted, I think, of five gentlemen. One of them was a representative of the employers. The late Government refused to place on that Royal Commission any representative of the workmen, and the consequence was that the workmen said, as I think they were entitled to say – This is not an impartial and fair Commission; it is not a Commission which there are all neutral members. It is a commission on which our antagonists . . . represented and we are not represented. Accordingly they refused to give any evidence or any assistance at all to that Royal Commission not with standing which the Royal Commission has reported, as I think can be maintained in support of three out . . . four of the principal parts of while this Bill is composed.

I now come to What is more important than the merits or demerits of the Government or the merits of the Opposition – namely, the merits of the Bill itself; and it is upon that, and that alone, that I ask your Lordships to concur. Some-one has said you never can understand anything in human affairs unless you understand how it grew, and I believe that to be true of this controversy. Trade unions are of old standing here, certainly 200 years. Until 1824 they were largely regulated by statute. After 1824 until 1871 they were principally left to the common law; and the tender mercies of the common law were cruel towards trade unions. Trade unions were held to be unlawful associations. A man could be indicted for belonging to them. It was held that strikes were unlawful transactions, and to such an extent did this penalising of these legitimate and useful associations proceed that it was decided in the year 1805 that a man could rob a trade union and embezzle its money with impunity.

These were great and heavy disabilities, but there was one thing that they could have for their advantage. In those dark days the funds of the trade unions were not liable to attack by any suitor in any Court. In the report of the Royal Commission there is an abstruse, and, if I may say so with great respect, a fine-spun discussion of the law upon that subject as it existed before 1871. The Royal Commission think that in theory the trade unions might be sued, but in practice it was impossible to sue them. I am not concerned to enter upon the reasons why they could not be sued, but this I affirm, and no man will contradict me, that from the dawn of English history there never had been any attempt to sue a trade union in order to reach its funds to pay damages to any one who was supposed to be wronged. Whether that was a law of procedure or a law of principle, I do not enter upon the discussion. I think it was a law of principle. It is sufficient to say there never had been, and until the decision of this House in the year 1901 there never was any attempt, even an unsuccessful attempt, to make trade unions liable for damages in any action. That was, at all events, one of the advantages that they enjoyed in the years prior to 1871.

I see near me noble Lords who took a distinguished part in the fight which arose in those days. When I first began to take an interest in public affairs there was a great movement for the purpose of placing trade unions upon a proper and legitimate footing, among the men who had complained of this hardship, of the unfair position in which they were placed, of the absence of protection by the law to legitimate combinations, and of the liability to be pillaged in secret and persecuted in open Court for things which are now universally recognised as lawful. A Royal Commission sat in 1869, and in the end the statutes of 1871 and 1875 were passed, embodying principles of protection for trade unions. The first claim was that trade unions should be legalised, so that no longer should their funds be liable to be stolen or their members prosecuted for belonging to a union. That was accomplished in 1871 by the great Statute passed by a Liberal Government. The effect of that

Act was not to incorporate trade unions, but to allow them to be registered with a sort of quasi-corporate existence, to protect their funds, and to prevent people from being prosecuted for belonging to them. That was the purpose of the Act.

But observe, from the commencement of the discussion down to the time when the Act received the Royal assent, there was not a whisper in this House or in the other, or in the public Press, or anywhere else, that there was to be any change in the old practice of the law by which trade unions were free from having their funds attacked. I wish to emphasise this point. It was never suggested, till the Act of 1871 was passed, that the immunity which trade unions had hitherto enjoyed from action was to be interfered with. If that was really the effect of the Act of 1871 it was the undesigned effect, for no one knew that it was being done. It was done by inadvertence and not by intention. In the year 1901 it was discovered for the first time by your Lordships' House, sitting judicially, that this Act of 1871 had had the effect of depriving the trade unions of the immunities which they had enjoyed in every previous period of English history. That was the decision in the celebrated Taft Vale ease. I am not presumptuous enough to suggest that that is not good law. I know the immense capacity and learning of the great Judges who so held. But it was accidental and undesigned law. The result is that that Act of 1871, which was intended to protect the trade unions and to be a boon to them, became a bane to them instead.

From the year 1871 to 1901 everyone believed that the law was still such that trade unions could not be sued; and when this House came to the other decision, they overruled the Court of Appeal, which had decided in accordance with the universal belief in the legal profession, and among men of business and workmen, that trade unions could not be sued. The world went on very well between 1871 and 1901. There was a great multitude of strikes; but search the records of Parliament and the Press, and you will not find that any one suggested that the law ought to be altered, and if this new proposal which is represented as so shocking is to be stigmatised as unjust, it is at least an injustice under which since 1871 the whole world of industry sat still without one complaint being made anywhere of the unfair operation of the law.

Trade unions, like the rest of the world, believed that the law was as I have said, and so believing they built up their great funds. From the Board of Trade Labour Gazette for March, 1906, I take the following particulars for the ten years between 1895 and 1904. During that time 100 principal trade unions spent £16,060,000, of which only 14 per cent, was spent on dispute pay, the rest being all spent upon benefits of various kinds All this was done in the belief that the law was as it had been in every antecedent period of English history; and then came the decision of this House in 1901 to say that the funds, painfully collected by half-crowns, shillings, and sixpences, were exposed to liability to be taken in satisfaction of damages. That is the case for the first part of the Bill. The purpose of this Bill is to place the law in the position in which every Englishman thought it was from the Norman Conquest onward up to the year 1901; and to prevent actions from being brought which never had been brought with success until that year. I submit that there may be some better reason that a craven compliance with the majority which induced the House of Commons to accept a proposal of this kind.

Now I come to the second proposal of the Bill. In the years 1871 to 1875 picketing, among other things, had been made difficult or dangerous by the decisions of the Courts of law. A great deal of indignation has been expressed against the practice of picketing. It is an extremely disagreeable thing, I have not the slightest doubt. It is a phase in an industrial war. What it means is this – and I do not wish to minimise the discomfort of the transaction – that the men watch at the entrance of the works or at other convenient places, for the purpose of endeavouring to prevent others from going in to take their places while a strike is in progress. It cannot be done without some measure of discomfort, although it can be done – and I am glad to think that it nearly always is done – without violence or intimidation. If it is done with violence or intimidation, your Lordships will never hear me say that it ought not to be properly punished.

But picketing is a thing which was legalised long ago by the law of England. It was legalised by the Act of 1859 which has since been repealed; and also it was legalised – and it is to the honour of the Conservative Government of that day that it was – by the Act of 1875. Lord Beaconsfield was the Prime Minister of that Government, and he was also the author of "Sybil," and a man with deep feelings on subjects of this kind. He sympathised with trade unions, as did Lord Cairns, one of the greatest Chancellors there has ever been in this country; and the third of the triumvirate responsible for the legislation of 1875 is the noble Viscount who is here now, Lord Cross. He will remember these transactions well, for he was Home Secretary, and if he corrects me, I shall know that I am wrong. But I think he will not correct me. The second claim of the workmen was that picketing should be put upon a proper footing; and it was by intention put upon a proper footing by the Act of 1875. It was legalised for the purpose of obtaining information.

When the Bill was passing through the House of Commons a Member moved an Amendment for the purpose of saying that picketing should be lawful, not merely for the purpose of obtaining information, but also for the purpose of peaceful persuasion; and the noble Viscount, being then Home Secretary, rose and said in the House of Commons, as will be seen from a reference to Hansard, that it was quite unnecessary to press the Amendment because, as the Bill stood, picketing would be lawful for the purposes of peaceful persuasion. In 1896 it was decided that picketing was only lawful for the purpose of obtaining information. The noble Viscount accepted what he was told by his advisers, and most innocently led the House not to proceed with the Amendment authorising picketing for peaceful persuasion, because he was advised that it was already the law of the land and that there was no necessity for the Amendment. Can your Lordships therefore complain that we have put in a clause making picketing lawful for the purpose of peaceful persuasion? It is another reason why the House of Commons may have thought that this Bill, notwithstanding the attacks of jurists and professors, which, I believe, have been very copious on this subject, had some merits and some title to be considered.

The third claim made by the workmen between 1871 and 1875 was that the law of conspiracy should be settled and made clear. They had suffered enough from the law of conspiracy. The law of conspiracy in this country is a very unsettled and a very difficult law to ascertain, and in regard to all subjects it would be better to have it cleared up. But the workmen said, "We want to have it cleared up in regard to trade unions alone." I have seen criticisms in regard to this Bill to the effect that it had been brought in only for one class. But then so was the Act of 1875 brought in for one class, and the noble Viscount (Viscount Cross), Lord Beaconsfield, and Lord Cairns introduced a clause in the Bill of 1875 dealing with this law of conspiracy for one class alone. They dealt with it in this way. At that time no one took any interest in the question of civil liability, and your Lordships will remember there never had been any attempt to make out any civil liability. It was only criminal liability that was thought of when an Amendment was being contemplated in the law of conspiracy. See what Lord Cairns, who certainly was not a revolutionary statesman, said – The principle on which the Bill was framed was that the offences in relation to trade disputes should be thoroughly known and understood, and that persons should not be subjected to the indirect and deluding action of the old law of conspiracy. I cannot use any more severe censure of the law of conspiracy. There was accordingly a clause inserted in the Bill that no persons in a case of trade dispute should be exposed to criminal punishment for conspiracy – Agreement or combination by two or more persons to do or procure to be done any act in contemplation or furtherance of a trade dispute between employer and workman shall not be indictable as conspiracy if the said act committed by one person would not be punishable as a crime. Then came the new world and the new ideas, and every one seemed to have forgotten all this controversy connected with the settlements of 1871 and 1875. Decisions were given to the effect that there was a civil liability, and therefore the civil responsibility for conspiracy became very serious. This Bill proposes to place civil responsibility for conspiracy on the same footing as criminal, nothing more nor less.

There is one other clause which is somewhat novel in point of matter. It is very technical and very difficult to enter upon except in the Committee stage, but I may give an illustration of the kind of case which is it intended to meet. There was the case of a strike where some Irishmen had been induced by the employers to come over to Whitehaven for the purpose of taking the places of the men who were out on strike. These Irishmen did not know that a strike was going on, and one of the officials of the trade union met them at the station and said to them – My men, do you know what yon are coming for? You are coming to replace your comrades who are on strike. I will pay your faros back again to Ireland. Will you go back? Not wishing to injure their comrades these men went back; but the trade union was held responsible and had to pay damages because it was interfering with a contract.

There was another case told to me by my friend, Mr. Shackleton, in which the hon. Member was himself concerned. It was a case in which men were working at standard wages, but the materials supplied by the employers were so bad that the men could not obtain their standard rate of wages. They struck, and other men came in answer to an advertisement which said that the standard rate of wages would be paid. The men knew nothing about the strike, but they were told that the statement about the standard rate of wages was wrong, because the materials were so bad that the standard rate of wages could not be earned. Those who advised the men were held responsible for correcting what was uncommonly like a fraud in the statement that the standard rate of wages was being paid. That is the class of case which is struck at by this fourth part of the Bill. The second, third, and fourth of the proposals I have indicated are in substance recommended by the Royal Commission, although the Royal Commission did not have the benefit of a single witness from the side of the workmen.

37

CINEMATOGRAPH ACT, 1909

Source: *Cinematograph Act*, 1909, 9 Ed. 7, c. 30

1. An exhibition of pictures or other optical effects by means of a cinematograph, or other similar apparatus, for the purposes of which inflammable films are used, shall not be given unless the regulations made by the Secretary of State for securing safety are complied with, or, save as otherwise expressly provided by this Act, elsewhere than in premises licensed for the purpose in accordance with the provisions of this Act. [Provision against cinematograph exhibition except in licensed premises.]

2. – (1) A county council may grant licences to such persons as they think fit to use the premises specified in the licence for the purposes aforesaid on such terms and conditions and under such restrictions as, subject to regulations of the Secretary of State, the council may by the respective licences determine. [Provisions as to licences.]

...

3. If the owner of a cinematograph or other apparatus uses the apparatus, or allows it to be used, or if the occupier of any premises allows those premises to be used, in contravention of the provisions of this Act or the regulations made thereunder, or of the conditions or restrictions upon or subject to which any licence relating to the premises has been granted under this Act, he shall be liable, on summary conviction, to a fine not exceeding twenty pounds, and in the case of a continuing offence to a further penalty of five pounds for each day during which the offence continues, and the licence (if any) shall be liable to be revoked by the county council. [Penalties.]

4. A constable or any officer appointed for the purpose by a county council may at all reasonable times enter any premises, whether licensed or not, in which he has reason to believe that such an exhibition as aforesaid is being or is about to be given, with a view to seeing whether the provisions of this Act, or any regulations made thereunder, and the conditions [Power of entry.]

of any licence granted under this Act, have been complied with, and, if any person prevents or obstructs the entry of a constable or any officer appointed as aforesaid, he shall be liable, on summary conviction, to a penalty not exceeding twenty pounds.

38

OFFICIAL SECRETS ACT, 1911

Source: *Official Secrets Act*, 1911, c. 28

1 PENALTIES FOR SPYING

(1) If any person for any purpose prejudicial to the safety or interests of the State –

    (a) approaches or is in the neighbourhood of, or enters any prohibited place within the meaning of this Act; or

    (b) makes any sketch, plan, model, or note which is calculated to be or might be or is intended to be directly or indirectly useful to an enemy; or

    (c) obtains or communicates to any other person any sketch, plan, model, article, or note, or other document or information which is calculated to be or might be or is intended to be directly or indirectly useful to an enemy;

he shall be guilty of felony, and shall be liable to penal servitude for any term not less than three years and not exceeding seven years.

(2) On a prosecution under this section, it shall not be necessary to show that the accused person was guilty of any particular act tending to show a purpose prejudicial to the safety or interests of the State, and, notwithstanding that no such act is proved against him, he may be convicted if, from the circumstances of the case, or his conduct, or his known character as proved, it appears that his purpose was a purpose prejudicial to the safety or interests of the State; and if any sketch, plan, model, article, note, document, or information relating to or used in any prohibited place within the meaning of this Act, or anything in such a place, is made, obtained, or communicated by any person other than a person acting under lawful authority, it shall be deemed to have been made, obtained, or communicated for a purpose prejudicial to the safety or interests of the State unless the contrary is proved.

2 WRONGFUL COMMUNICATION, &C. OF INFORMATION

(1) If any person having in his possession or control any sketch, plan, model, article, note, document, or information which relates to or is used in a prohibited place or anything in such a place, or which has been made or obtained in

contravention of this Act, or which. has been entrusted in confidence to him by any person holding office under His Majesty or which he has obtained owing to his position as a person who holds or has held office under His Majesty, or as a person who holds or has held a contract made on behalf of his Majesty, or as a person who is or has been employed under a person who holds or has held such an office or contract, –

(a) communicates the sketch, plan, model, article, note, document, or information to any person, other than a person to whom he is authorised to communicate it, or a person to whom it is in the interest of the State his duty to communicate it, or

(b) retains the sketch, plan, model, article, note, or document in his possession or control when he has no right to retain it or when it is contrary to his duty to retain it:

that person shall be guilty of a misdemeanour.

(2) If any person receives any sketch, plan, model, article, note, document, or information, knowing, or having reasonable ground to believe, at the time when he receives it, that the sketch, plan, model, article, note, document, or information is communicated to him in contravention of this Act, he shall be guilty of a misdemeanour, unless he proves that the communication to him of the sketch, plan, model, article, note, document, or information was contrary to his desire.

(3) A person guilty of a misdemeanour under this section shall be liable to imprisonment with or without hard labour for a term not exceeding two years, or to a fine, or to both imprisonment and a fine.

3   DEFINITION OF PROHIBITED PLACE

For the purposes of this Act, the expression "prohibited place" means –

(a) any work of defence, arsenal, factory, dockyard, camp, ship, telegraph or signal station, or office belonging to His Majesty, and any other place belonging to His Majesty used for the purpose of building, repairing, making, or storing any ship, arms, or other materials or instruments of use in time of war, or any plans or documents relating thereto; and

(b) any place not belonging to His Majesty where any ship, arms, or other materials or instruments of use in time of war, or any plans or documents relating thereto, are being made, repaired, or stored under contract with, or with any person on behalf of, His Majesty, or otherwise on behalf of His Majesty; and

(c) any place belonging to His Majesty which is for the time being declared by a Secretary of State to be a prohibited place for the purposes of this section on the ground that information with respect thereto, or damage thereto, would be useful to an enemy; and

(d) any railway, road, way, or channel, or other means of communication by land or water (including any works or structures being part thereof or connected therewith), or any place used for gas, water, or electricity works or other works for purposes of a public character, or any place where any ship, arms, or other materials or instruments of use in time of war, or any plans or documents relating thereto, are being made, repaired, or stored otherwise than on behalf of His Majesty, which is for the time being declared by a Secretary of State to be a prohibited place for the purposes of this section, on the ground that information with respect thereto, or the destruction or obstruction thereof, or interference therewith, would be useful to an enemy.

39

DEFENCE OF THE REALM ACT, 1914

Source: *Defence of the Realm Act*, 1914, 4 & 5 Geo. 5, c. 29

An Act to confer on His Majesty in Council power to make Regulations during the present War for the Defence of the Realm. [8th August 1914.]

A.D. 1914.

BE it enacted by the King's most Excellent Majesty, by and with the advice and consent of the Lords Spiritual and Temporal, and Commons, in this present Parliament assembled, and by the authority of the same, as follows:

Power to make regulations.

1. His Majesty in Council has power during the continuance of the present war to issue regulations as to the powers and duties of the Admiralty and Army Council, and of the members of His Majesty's forces, and other persons acting in His behalf, for securing the public safety and the defence of the realm; and may, by such regulations, authorise the trial by courts martial and punishment of persons contravening any of the provisions of such regulations designed –

(*a*) to prevent persons communicating with the enemy or obtaining information for that purpose or any purpose calculated to jeopardise the success of the operations of any of His Majesty's forces or to assist the enemy; or

(*b*) to secure the safety of any means of communication, or of railways, docks or harbours;

in like manner as if such persons were subject to military law and had on active service committed an offence under section five of the Army Act.

Short title.

2. This Act may be cited as the Defence of the Realm Act, 1914.

40

EMERGENCY POWERS ACT, 1920

Source: *Emergency Powers Act*, 1920, 10 & 11 Geo. 5, c. 55

An Act to make exceptional provision for the Protection of the Community in cases of Emergency. [29th October 1920.]

A.D. 1920.

BE it enacted by the King's most Excellent Majesty, by and with the advice and consent of the Lords Spiritual and Temporal, and Commons, in this present Parliament assembled, and by the authority of the same, as follows:

1. – (1) If at any time it appears to His Majesty that any action has been taken or is immediately threatened by any persons or body of persons of such a nature and on so extensive a scale as to be calculated, by interfering with the supply and distribution of food, water, fuel, or light, or with the means of locomotion, to deprive the community, or any substantial portion of the community, of the essentials of life, His Majesty may, by proclamation (hereinafter referred to as a proclamation of emergency), declare that a state of emergency exists.

Issue of proclamations of emergency.

No such proclamation shall be in force for more than one month, without prejudice to the issue of another proclamation at or before the end of that period.

(2) Where a proclamation of emergency has been made, the occasion thereof shall forthwith be communicated to Parliament, and, if Parliament is then separated by such adjournment or prorogation as will not expire within five days, a proclamation shall be issued for the meeting of Parliament within five days, and Parliament shall accordingly meet and sit upon the day appointed by that proclamation, and shall continue to sit and act in like manner as if it had stood adjourned or prorogued to the same day.

2. – (1) Where a proclamation of emergency has been made, and so long as the proclamation is in force, it shall be lawful for His Majesty in Council, by Order, to make regulations for securing the essentials of life to the community, and those regulations may confer or impose on a Secretary of State or other Government department, or any other persons in His Majesty's service or acting on His Majesty's behalf, such powers and duties

Emergency regulations.

as His Majesty may deem necessary for the preservation of the peace, for securing and regulating the supply and distribution of food, water, fuel, light, and other necessities, for maintaining the means of transit or locomotion, and for any other purposes essential to the public safety and the life of the community, and may make such provisions incidental to the powers aforesaid as may appear to His Majesty to be required for making the exercise of those powers effective:

Provided that nothing in this Act shall be construed to authorise the making of any regulations imposing any form of compulsory military service or industrial conscription:

Provided also that no such regulation shall make it an offence for any person or persons to take part in a strike, or peacefully to persuade any other person or persons to take part in a strike.

(2) Any regulations so made shall be laid before Parliament as soon as may be after they are made, and shall not continue in force after the expiration of seven days from the time when they are so laid unless a resolution is passed by both Houses providing for the continuance thereof.

(3) The regulations may provide for the trial, by courts of summary jurisdiction, of persons guilty of offences against the regulations; so, however, that the maximum penalty which may be inflicted for any offence against any such regulations shall be imprisonment with or without hard labour for a term of three months, or a fine of one hundred pounds, or both such imprisonment and fine, together with the forfeiture of any goods or money in respect of which the offence has been committed: Provided that no such regulations shall alter any existing procedure in criminal cases, or confer any right to punish by fine or imprisonment without trial.

(4) The regulations so made shall have effect as if enacted in this Act, but may be added to, altered, or revoked by resolution of both Houses of Parliament or by regulations made in like manner and subject to the like provisions as the original regulations; and regulations made under this section shall not be deemed to be statutory rules within the meaning of section one of the Rules Publication Act, 1893.

| 56 & 57 Vict. c. 66. |

(5) The expiry or revocation of any regulations so made shall not be deemed to have affected the previous operation thereof, or the validity of any action taken thereunder, or any penalty or punishment incurred in respect of any contravention or failure to comply therewith, or any proceeding or remedy in respect of any such punishment or penalty.

| Short title and application. |

3. – (1) This Act may be cited as the Emergency Powers Act, 1920.

(2) This Act shall not apply to Ireland.

41

REPORT OF THE BROADCASTING COMMITTEE, 1925
Summary of Recommendations

Source: London: Her Majesty's Stationery Office, 1925, pp. 14–16

20. Our principal recommendations are as follows:

(a) That the broadcasting service should be conducted by a public corporation acting as Trustee for the national interest, and that its status and duties should correspond with those of a public service

(b) That the corporation should either be set up by Act of Parliament or be incorporated under the 'Companies Acts, limited by Guarantee, and dispensing with the word "Limited"; that in either case the corporation should hold the licence of the Postmaster-General for a period of not less than ten years;

(c) That the corporation should be known as the "British Broadcasting Commission"; that it should consist of not more than seven or less than five Commissioners, all nominated by the Crown, the first Commissioners to hold office for five years; that the Commissioners should be persons of judgment and independence, free of commitments, with business acumen and experienced in affairs; that one of the Commissioners might, if thought desirable, be one of the existing members of the British Broadcasting Company; that the Commissioners should have the power to appoint an Executive Commissioner with a seat on the Board; that all Commissioners should be adequately remunerated;

(d) That the Commissioners should appoint, in consultation with appropriate Societies and Organisations, as many Advisory Committees as are necessary to ensure due consideration of all phases of broadcasting;

(e) That the entire property and undertaking of the British Broadcasting Company as a going concern should be vested in the Commission on the 1st January, 1927; that all existing contracts and staff of the British Broadcasting Company should be taken over by the new Commission;

(f) That the Postmaster-General should remain the licensing authority and be responsible for collecting the licence fees; that the detection and prosecution of those who conceal their equipment should be vigorously pursued;

(g) That the provision for experiment and research should be generous;

(h) That the Commission should be empowered to raise capital;

(i) That the fee of ten shillings for a receiver's licence should be maintained; that the first charge on the Revenue from licence fees 'should be the expenditure incurred by the Postmaster-General in connection with the Broadcasting service; that after paying the Commissioners an income thoroughly adequate to enable them to ensure the full and efficient maintenance and development of the service; any surplus should be retained by the State;

(j) That the Commission's accounts should be reviewed by the Comptroller and Auditor General;

(k) That so soon as the licence expires or is withdrawn the Commission, on due prevision being made for the discharge of all debts and liabilities, should be bound to transfer or dispose of its whole undertaking in such manner as the Postmaster-General may direct;

(l) That the Commissioners should be entitled to all the ordinary rights as regards the use of copyright material – whether in news or otherwise – and that it is unnecessary to invest them with any special privilege or preference;

(m) That the claims of those listeners who desire a larger proportion of educational matter, though relatively few in number, should, if possible, be met;

(n) That every effort should be made to raise the standard of style and performance in every phase of broadcasting and particularly in music;

(o) That a moderate amount of controversial matter should be broadcast, provided the material is of high quality and distributed with scrupulous fairness; and that the discretion of the Commissioners in this connection should he upheld;

(p) That licences should be granted to blind persons free of charge;

(q) That the prestige and status of the Commission should be freely acknowledged and their sense of responsibility emphasised; that, although Parliament must retain the right of ultimate control and the Postmaster-General must be the Parliamentary Spokesman on broad questions of policy, the Commissioners should be invested with the maximum of freedom which Parliament is prepared to concede;

(r) That the Commissioners should present an annual Report to Parliament.

42

'TRADE DISPUTES AND TRADE UNIONS BILL'

Ellen Wilkinson

Source: House of Commons, 5 May 1927

I find it a little difficult to follow the excellent speech which has been made by the hon. Member opposite, in view of his concluding remarks, because I am afraid he will go from this House to his constituency and say that not only did the women follow him at his election . . . but, alas, they followed him in this House also. I am afraid the hon. Member's remarks with regard to women Members are rather like his remarks with regard to trade unionism in general; they are rather old-fashioned. While we respect his grey hairs and the long work he has put in in the trade unionist movement, we realise that he speaks for a past generation. Previous speakers have pointed out many peculiar features of this Bill, including the new crimes which have been created, and the general feeling of uncertainty which will be left as to what trade unionists will or will not be able to do. The most amazing thing about both the Debate in this House and the advocacy of the Bill in the country has been the curious misunderstanding of working-class psychology shown by the Tory party. I think the hon. Member for Yardley (Mr. Jephcott) understands that very much better than many of those who have spoken with him. They do not realise that though trade unionists may grumble, that though minorities may want this or that alteration, the trade unions which have been built up during more than a century are a very sacred thing indeed to the working classes of this country.

I am going to ask certain hon. Members of this House, such as the hon. Member for Stockton (Captain Macmillan), the hon. Member for Oldham (Mr. Duff Cooper), and other hon. Members for working-class constituencies, whether it is not the fact that while minorities here and there are prepared to grumble, the mass of trade unionists are extremely suspicious when employers show any considerable interest in their trade union. I want to give an illustration of that from a side of this question which has not yet been touched on in this Debate. A prominent supporter of the Government, addressing a large meeting of women about this Bill, made the following statement: The Government will protect the working class wife and mother from having her income suddenly interrupted by wild cat folly like the general strike; and will protect her and her husband if they decide together that he shall work and not strike. This Bill will protect her and hers from hatred, ridicule and contempt. I have already heard a Conservative meeting for working women addressed on those lines. It is rather from the point of view of the working women and their attitude with regard to the Bill that I wish to speak.

The working women of this country would be exceedingly glad to have some protection from this Government. They would like some protection from the profiteer; they would like some protection from the price-fixing associations, about whom evidence has been given before the Food Council, who are able to raise the price of food in a time when wages are low; they would like protection from such associations as were referred to by an hon. Member who spoke about farmers pouring milk down the drains rather than allow it to be sold at a low price. These are all things done by employers' trade unions, but there is not one word in this Bill as to how the women are to be protected in that respect.

They are to be protected from intimidation. I can understand a woman being very much upset when a crowd of men come round her house at night because her husband is going to work, but I can understand her being still more upset when the employer sends his foreman or his manager, as was done in a very large number of cases during the recent coal dispute, to tell that woman that, unless she persuades her husband to go to work, there will be no more work for her husband or her son, and that she will have to leave the tied cottage, which belongs to the colliery. While I admit that a number of men round your house may be unpleasant, it is much more serious intimidation to go into that woman's house and tell her that there is not going to be any more work for her husband or her son unless she brings influence upon her husband to persuade him to go to work. It is very curious that the Government should only want to protect a working woman from her fellow working men, that they should only want to protect a woman from the organisation that exists to improve her husband's wages and conditions. If, as the Tory party say, this Bill is to be a charter of protection for the workingwoman, let us have protection all round. Let us give her protection from the employer who reduces her husband's wages and increase her prices. There is not one single word of that protection in this Bill.

I would like to know how this protection is going to be given. The Attorney-General and the Solicitor-General are very clever men, and it may be possible for them, though I do not know how they are going to do it, to deal with the case of men meeting in a public house, such as the right hon Gentleman the Member for Colne Valley (Mr. Snowden) referred to. I would like to ask the Solicitor-General, since he is here, how he proposes to protect the wife of a blackleg and the blackleg himself from the hatred, contempt and ridicule of the women in a mining village, or anywhere else where there is a large strike? How is he going to force Mrs. Striker to speak to Mrs. Blackleg if she does not wish to do so? Are the local police to keep lists of the number of times Mrs. Brown asked Mrs. Jones to tea previous to a dispute and the number of times she asks her afterwards? Are we going to have policemen calling on the wife of a striker and saying, "Mrs. Brown is in tears because you are not asking her to tea any more. You did it before the strike, and unless you ask her to tea you are bringing her into hatred, ridicule and contempt. She is very much upset about it, and unless you ask her to tea you will have to go to prison." I would like to ask the Attorney-General whether he proposes to send policemen into the sewing meeting of the local church? I have attended those functions, and I know something about them, and I can imagine that the wife of a striker and the wife of a blackleg will have a distinctly unhappy time.

I regret that the Solicitor-General is not prepared to enlighten us on these important matters, but I would like to know whether there are any means by which the ladies congregated round the church sewing-machine can be prevented from showing their hatred, ridicule and contempt of the woman whose husband has gone to work and so helped to break a strike for better wages. I do not know whether we are going to have a new Tory commandment added to the Ten Commandments: "Thou shalt love the neighbour that tries to take the bread from thy children's mouths." If that is the position of the Tory party, they are going to have an extraordinary difficult time. They can legislate against overt crimes, but I cannot see how they are going to legislate against people showing their feelings towards those who are attempting to break a dispute when the men are engaged in what they believe is a fight for their lives.

I was very much struck by a remark made by a woman in my constituency when I was pointing out that one might be sent to prison for calling a man a blackleg. She said, "Oh, well, that does not matter, we will call him a Douglas Hogg." That raises a very interesting point. Suppose a bench of magistrates were dealing with a striker who had called a blackleg a "Douglas Hogg." Would the magistrates decide that it was a term of ridicule or contempt? It will be a very difficult position for men who have any respect for our learned Attorney-General, and I have no doubt whatever that that woman's phrase is likely to be current in any dispute of the kind.

Tory speakers in this Debate have said the working class are not excited about this Bill. I think that on the whole that is rather true, but I think it is because they know perfectly well that this Bill will not work. If they want to strike they will strike, and nothing we can do will prevent them. It may be asked, "Then why this opposition to the Bill?" It is because when you get a Bill like this the danger lies in the fear of petty tyranny towards the obscure man. It is not men like my right hon. Friend the Member for Derby (Mr. Thomas), or the right hon. Gentleman the Member for Colne Valley (Mr. Snowden) or the right hon. Gentleman the Member for Aberavon (Mr. Ramsay MacDonald), or even Mr. A. J. Cook, who are the victims of a Government at the time of a dispute. During the late dispute the safest person in this country was Arthur Cook, because the Government knew perfectly well what would be the effect of putting a man like that in prison. The whole difficulty centres round the obscure man, the man in the little village, the man who is at the mercy of every small informer and his wife. When I was going round hundreds of small mining villages in my capacity as a member of the Miners' Relief Committee, I saw the amount of petty tyranny that was going on, the number of people who went round to the police and said, "So-and-so has called me a blackleg." Even then men and women were put in prison because it was said they had intimidated others . . .

The hon. Member who spoke before me said that women always break their word. I do not propose to break mine. I would like to say, in conclusion, that the Conservative party as a whole has entirely misunderstood the psychology of the working classes. There are men like the previous speaker who are the malcontents, the minority, but, if you have a great wave of working-class feeling like you had last May on the part of men who were not concerned with coercing any Government but who were concerned in showing their sympathy with the miners – if you have that spirit again, you will have the same result, not because the leaders want it, or because the men consciously want it, but because you have a great mass wave of sympathy that nothing is going to prevent. If, as the result of that, you put 5,000,000 working men in prison, you will have 5,000,000 working women behind them ready to go too.

INDEX

Address of the Committee to the People of England (Administrative Reform Association) 51–52

alcohol 72–75
Aliens Act, 1905 134–136
Annual Holiday Bill 90–92
Astor, Nancy 72–75

Bhownaggree, Mancherjee 71
Bondfield, Margaret 82–85
Bradlaugh, Charles 123–129
British Constitution, The (Marx) 12
broadcasting 151–152
Bulwer, Edward Lytton 117–122
Burdett-Coutts, William 123
Butler, H. P. 90
bye-election policy 55–56
Byron, Lord 5–9

Case of Wolf Tone 98–99
Catholics 115–116
Cinematograph Act, 1909 143–144
Combination Act, 1800 100–102
'Concerning Government' (Morris) 15–18
Conway, M. 85
Cook, A. J. 155
Cooper, Duff 57, 153
Corn Laws 12
Crewe-Milnes, Robert 55
Crisis of Liberalism, The: New Issues of Democracy (Hobson) 19–21

Debate on the Address (Bondfield) 82–85
Debate on the Address (Saklatvala) 77–81
Defence of the Realm Act, 1914 148
democracy 19–21
Disraeli, Benjamin 13–14
Duncombe, Thomas 44–50

Emergency Powers Act, 1920 149–150

Fox, Charles James 95–96
Framework Bill 5–9

Habeas Corpus Suspension Act, 1794 97
Habeas Corpus Suspension Bill 108–111
Hadfield, Gorge 68
Hobson, J. A. 19–21
Hotham, Beaumont 68
Housing (Revision of Contributions) Bill (Rathbone) 86–89

immigration 134–136
Indian Taxation 71
Ireland 46, 49, 78–80, 112, 121, 127, 135, 150

Jessel, George 131

Labour party 56, 79
Liberalism 13–14, 19–21
Liberal party 13–14, 55–57, 138
Liquor Traffic (Restrictions) (Astor) 72–75
Lloyd George, David 90
London Corresponding Society 26–28
Loreburn, Lord 137–142

Macmillan, Chrystal 60–61, 153
Marx, Karl 12
Masque of Anarchy (Shelley) 29–43
Mersey Docks Trustees v. Gibbs 131
Morris, William 15–18

National Women's Social and Political Union (NWSPU) 55–59
Newspaper Stamp Duties 117–122

Official Secrets Act, 1911 145–147

Pankhurst, Christabel 55–59
partial privileges 27–28
People's Charter - Petition (Duncombe) 44–50
Phillips, Marion 90–92
Poor Law 12
Public Meetings in the Metropolis (Bradlaugh) 123–129

Rathbone, Eleanor 86–89
Reid, Robert 137–142
religion 95–96, 115–116
Religious Liberty (Fox) 95–96
Rentoul, G. 90
Repeal of the *Test and Corporation Acts*, 1828 112–114
Report of the Broadcasting Committee 151–152
representation: in Astor 72–75; in Bhownaggree 71; in Bondfield 82–85; in Phillips 90–92; in Rathbone 86–89; in Rothschild 65–70; in Saklatvala 77–81; in Wintringham 76
Rigby v. Connell 131
Roman Catholic Emancipation Act, 1829 115–116
Romilly, Samuel 108–111
Rothschild, Baron Lionel Nathan de 65–70
Royal Parks and Pleasure Gardens (Wintringham) 76
Russell, John 65, 67
Ry. Co. v. London, Chatham and Dover Ry. Co. 131

Saklatvala, Shapurji 77–81
secrets, official 145–147

Secularism in Its Various Relations 53–54
Shelley, Percy Bysshe 29–43
Sheridan, Richard 103–107
Slum Clearance Bill 87–88
Smith, J. A. 65, 67
Society for Constitutional Information 25
Somerville, D. G. 85
Speech at Crystal Palace (Disraeli) 13–14
Spooner, Richard 69
Standing Order for the Exclusion of Strangers 103–107
state secrets 145–147
Struggle for Political Liberty, The (Macmillan) 60–61

Taff Vale Case 130–133
taxes 71, 117–122
Tennyson, Alfred 10–11
Test and Corporation Acts, 1828 112–114
Tone, Wolf 98–99
Tory Party 13–14, 57, 153–155
Trade Disputes and Trade Unions Bill 153–156
Trade Disputes Bill 137–142
Trade Union Acts 130

Vindication of the Rights of Woman (Wollstonecraft) 3–4

Walpole, Spencer 66, 68–69
Walter, J. Tudor 87
Warren, Charles 65–67, 128
Watts, Charles 53–54
Wilkinson, Ellen 153–156
Wintringham, Margaret 76
Wollstonecraft, Mary 3–4
women 3–4, 55–61, 76
Women's Social and Political Union 55–59

You Ask Me, Why, Tho' Ill At Ease 10–11